IMAGES
of America

BUILDING BARTLESVILLE
1945–2000

IMAGES
of America

BUILDING BARTLESVILLE

1945–2000

Scott W. Perkins

ARCADIA
PUBLISHING

Published by Arcadia Publishing
Charleston, South Carolina

Library of Congress Catalog Card Number: 2007921382

For all general information contact Arcadia Publishing at:
Telephone 843-853-2070
Fax 843-853-0044
E-mail sales@arcadiapublishing.com
For customer service and orders:
Toll-Free 1-888-313-2665

Visit us on the Internet at www.arcadiapublishing.com

*Dedicated to my fellow interpreters of Bartlesville history,
especially those who volunteer their time and talents
in welcoming our friends from far and near.*

CONTENTS

ACKNOWLEDGMENTS

Since my first visit to Bartlesville in 2004, and after making it my home two years later, I have experienced the continued warmth and kindness of its citizens. In my role as curator of collections and exhibitions at Price Tower Arts Center, many Bartians share with me their experiences of having worked in, stayed in, dined at, or toured the Price Tower over its lifetime. For them, and my colleagues at Price Tower Arts Center, this book is dedicated. Kay Johnson, Laura Riley, Jennifer Cordero, Libby Leonard, Deshane Atkins, Christine Staton, and Cynthia Naylor cheered me on throughout this project, as did our former executive director Richard Townsend.

Our corps of 40 volunteers and docents must be acknowledged for welcoming nearly 30,000 visitors to our building each year, and thus Bartlesville. I thank especially Joyce O'Donnell for her knowledge of Bartlesville history and Dan O'Donnell and Mark Dreiling who photographed many of the original drawings used herein.

The Bartlesville Area History Museum (Karen Wood-Smith, Jo Crabtree, Kay Little, and Gary Nealis), the ConocoPhillips Corporate Archives (Jenny Brown and Kathy Triebel), the Bartlesville Community Center (Pat Patterson), and the Frank Phillips Home (Jim Goss and Kim Goss) provided images of Bartlesville's landmarks and I value fully the collegiality and commitment our institutions hold in preserving our city's cultural history. Without them, and their photographic archives, this book would not have been possible.

Ambler Architects (Scott Ambler and Kathy White) allowed me to view and photograph the yet unstudied work of Tom McCrory, as well as the work of their own important firm. Margo Stipe at the Frank Lloyd Wright Archives provided images of Wright's only Bartlesville residence, and Mary Woolever of the Ryerson and Burnham Libraries at the Art Institute of Chicago assisted with photographs of Bruce Goff's architecture, while Bonnie Eggert gave me an excellent tour of Goff's Education Building for the Redeemer Lutheran Church.

Ann Marie Lonsdale and Ted Gerstle, my editors at Arcadia Publishing, were especially patient and understanding of the difficulties surrounding my first publication. Finally, I thank my family for sustaining me through many endeavors with their confidence and support.

INTRODUCTION

In 2006, Price Tower, Frank Lloyd Wright's only realized skyscraper, celebrated its 50th anniversary. From the research and resulting exhibition surrounding that commemoration came a better understanding of the impact "modern" architecture had upon the "rural" downtown of Bartlesville in the middle of the 20th century. As only one of hundreds of structures built in Bartlesville since World War II, it maintains its remarkable presence upon the skyline and seduces visitors with its angularity and intriguing materials.

But it is not alone.

The architectural climate in Bartlesville following World War II was ripe with experimentation and innovations. Census records show the city's population more than doubled, from 16,243 people in 1940 to 34,748 at the end of the 20th century, and while the oil industry may have sparked this growth, it was the social and cultural offerings that gave Bartlesville its hometown atmosphere and vibrancy for those who stayed. Considering its size, Bartlesville's architectural heritage overall is diverse and represents nearly every style and level of taste, in both commercial and residential forms. Some buildings were designed by famous architects and firms with global reputations, others by those with regional acclaim. Those meeting commercial, educational, or public service needs were often built in the light of economic booms while residential architecture was more frequently designed as part of housing planning initiatives that expanded Bartlesville's boundaries in nearly every direction.

Beginning an architectural history at 1945, then, may seem effortless. For many, the past 60 years can easily be summed up as modern or contemporary in scope, but in fact architecture of this period is more complex as ever-improving advances in construction materials, engineering, and technology impacted the way buildings were designed and constructed. Shifting roles of men and women both at home and in the workplace affected the ways in which buildings were designed during this time as did the introduction of computers, fax machines, and televisions—not to mention the growing reliance upon the automobile as a means of transporting people between buildings.

These types of influences also caused a shift in the perception of architecture over time, often posing the question, "What should this building *do*?" Once the basic functional provision of shelter is met, many of a building's features become decorative and the concept of "style" becomes increasingly important. Those such as the Bartlesville Community Center and Price Tower have become almost iconic, their forms used to signify Bartlesville as a community, while others, especially the residential works, took on the particular (or idiosyncratic) characteristic traits of their patrons. Patrons of architect Bruce Goff sought out his ability to meet to not only the needs of modern life, but to utilize innovative materials to provide their homes with an individualistic appearance, often including original works of decorative art and built-in furnishings.

Buildings of all types, however, are habitually assigned attributes by differing user groups, depending upon their relationships within them. Homes are remodeled to remove features deemed unlivable by their new owners, with alterations such as a new garage, expanded kitchen, or additional bedrooms affecting the previous design. School children and teachers, doctors and patients, and executives and custodial crews each have varying degrees of appreciation for architecture within their respective environments—each person's interaction adding to the building's meaning.

The architectural experience has also become more important in understanding one's culture and social world. The best way to do this, of course, is first-hand and only by touching it, seeing it, and walking through it can architecture best be appreciated. Light, sound, and psychological moods are altered within it, as are relationships with the natural environment through its materials, temperature controls, landscape plantings, and spatial arrangements. The need for an "authentic" experience has propelled an industry of bed-and-breakfast inns, historic home museums, and informative guides to cultural sites the world over. This budding "architourism" movement is revealing, and has made a valuable cultural and economic impact upon the city, most recently through the National Trust for Historic Preservation's selection of Bartlesville as one of their Dozen Distinctive Destinations for 2006.

As new buildings continue to rise in Bartlesville, they too will become part of the fabric of the "City of Legends's" architectural legacy. The close of the 20th century now allows architecture historians to reflect on the past century and honor those buildings that are felt to be worthy of saving, preserving, and celebrating. As of October 2007, there were but four buildings in Bartlesville listed on the National Register of Historic Places—the residence of Frank Phillips; the former Washington County Courthouse; La Quinta, the residence of H. V. Foster (now Oklahoma Wesleyan University); and Price Tower, the only design after 1945 and the only building subsequently designated as a national historic landmark. Neither of these landmarks are located within the Bartlesville Downtown Historic District, itself honored by the National Trust for Historic Preservation in 1991 and bounded by Second Street, Cherokee Avenue, Fourth Street, and the Atchison, Topeka, and Santa Fe Railroad (AT&SF) tracks.

Recent publications such as Karen Smith Woods's 1999 book *Bartlesville*, part of Arcadia Publishing's Postcard History Series, is an excellent companion as it offers glimpses not only into Bartlesville's pre-statehood years and earlier architectural history, but serves to prove that architecture, even in an ephemeral souvenir form, is worthy of preserving. The Bartlesville Area History Museum has organized walking tours of many of Bartlesville's downtown historic buildings, permitting tourists and architecture aficionados the opportunity to stroll through the past, and the curators and docents of historic homes and buildings, including the Frank Phillips Home, La Quinta, and Price Tower, incorporate architectural history into their interpretation of interiors, exhibitions, and artifacts.

Inherent in any published study of a city's buildings is the fact that not all aspects of architecture can be presented. While the 33 architectural projects included in this publication make that attempt, *Building Bartlesville* leaves many stories untold. The research completed for this volume alone made it apparent that some buildings are in danger of being forgotten, as they continually become altered, demolished, uncared for, or remain undocumented in either word or image. It is with hope, then, that the following pages serve to honor the men and women who have helped to build Bartlesville, as well as those who are continuing to protect, conserve, and interpret its architectural legacy.

One

NEW MATERIALS, NEW IDEAS

THE "MODERN" BARTLESVILLE HOME

From bungalow to ranch, apartment to villa, prefab to free-form, the residential architecture of Bartlesville is as diverse as its community. Over the past six decades, a decidedly expressive collection of "modern" homes have made their mark on the city's history and a few upon architectural history in general. This chapter introduces the patrons and architects of some of Bartlesville's most interesting residential architecture and explores the varied forms and materials used in its construction.

Building a home in Bartlesville, especially an architect-designed home, was filled with near limitless possibilities. Land was not difficult to come by, and for those patrons with the means to do so, a residence could be well-incorporated into the Oklahoma prairie landscape. Subdivisions sprouted up to give home builders additional options, and tree-lined streets to the south and west of downtown Bartlesville soon were filled with designs of all styles. Pockets of mid-century and postwar architecture soon blossomed.

The act of commissioning a home—designing it in conjunction with an architect to meet specific parameters and wishes—is not a new concept. However, for the patrons of architects such as Bruce Goff, the resulting design often exceeded expectations and placed it within a unique pocket of "mid-century modernism." Goff's aesthetic ranged from minimalist to sculpturally organic, more often dictated by his clients' taste than his own, yet each a decidedly different type of engineered structure. More common of the era were homes such as those designed by Cliff May and Thomas McCrory, who drew upon the conventions of popular architecture without making their homes seems at all conventional.

Bartlesville native Scott Ambler, represented in this chapter by a project he designed for his family, is both architect and patron, his postmodern design the opportunity to infuse historical influences into a home built near the dawn of a new century. As an architect known for adaptive reuse and preservation of historic Bartlesville properties, Ambler's firm plays a significant role in the legacy of many of the buildings in these pages.

Harold and Mary Lou Patteson Price purchased land southeast of downtown Bartlesville as a ranch on which to raise horses. The property, known as Star View Farm, would be the site of not only their ranch-style home, designed by Los Angeles architect Cliff May, but of homes for both their sons. (Courtesy of the Frank Phillips Home.)

Star View Farm's large pond made for a fine view from the house and toward the two areas where each of the Price sons would build homes. Harold Jr. commissioned Frank Lloyd Wright to design a home for his family to the southwest, and brother Joe commissioned Bruce Goff to design a bachelor studio that later grew to become Shin'enKan, to the northeast. (Courtesy of Price Tower Arts Center Archives.)

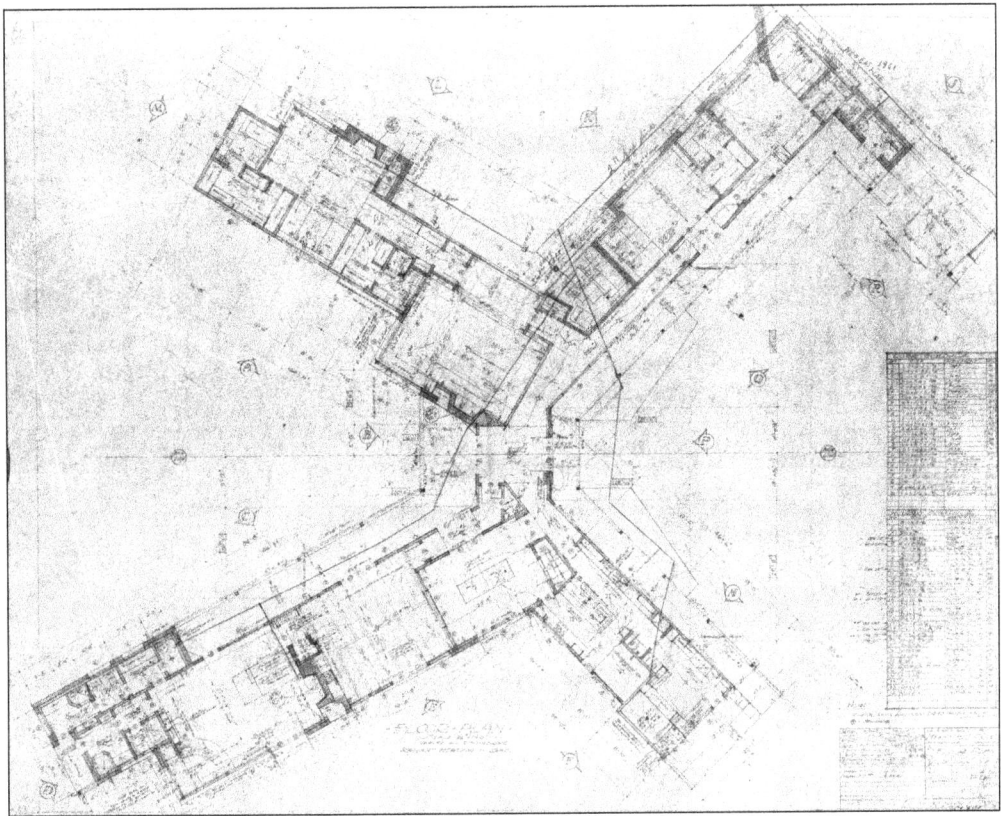

The X-shape of May's 1946 plan was hardly usual and consisted of four arms, the ends of two connecting to the garage by a pair of covered drives. The entire plan of the home was drawn on two sheets—the upper showing the four-armed structure and the one at right showing the garage and connection points to the right-most arms, creating an octagonal motor court accessed via the covered driveways. (Courtesy of Price Tower Arts Center Archives.)

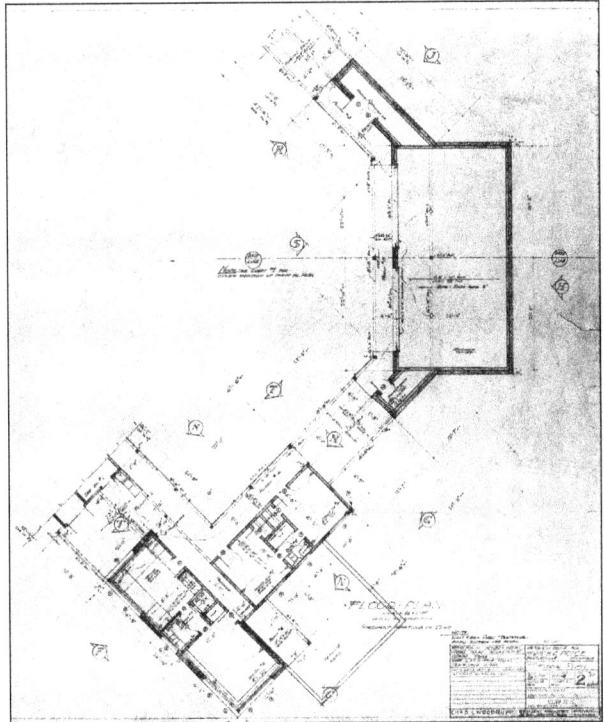

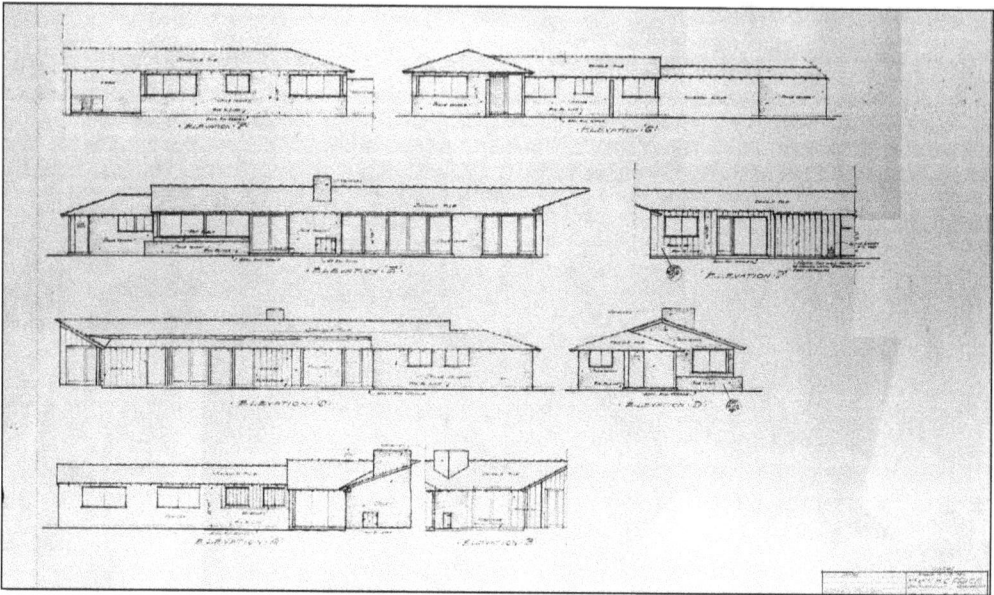

Cliff May engaged Bartlesville architect Charles Woodruff as the resident architect for the Star View Farm project, and it was his job to prepare final documents for the contractor. The elevation drawings of the Prices' residence provided locations of doors and the home's numerous windows as well as the details of the exterior building materials specified by May for the scheme. The low, horizontal profile of the home, with shallow roofline emblematic of the ranch style, was finished with stone veneers, painted board and batten, and painted plaster. Flagstone was specified for the porches surrounding the home, and slate tile was applied as roofing. (Courtesy of Price Tower Arts Center Archives.)

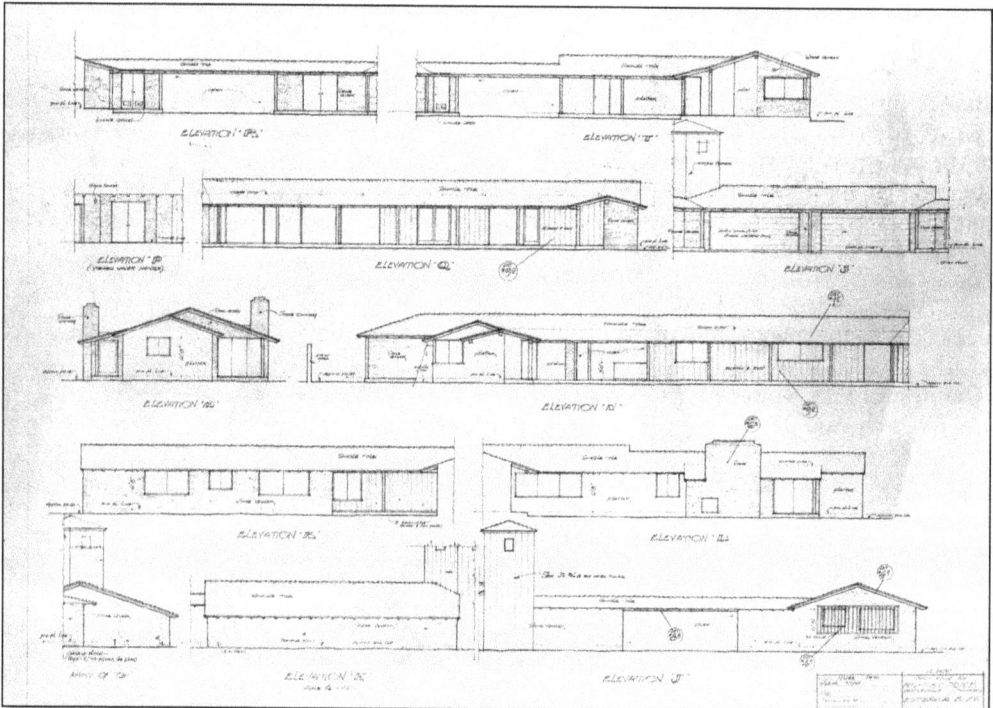

Two views of the Prices' residence at Star View Farm show the inner motor court and the family's cars through one of the covered drives. To the left, in the upper photograph, were the garage and a water tower capped with a horse-shaped weather vane, an indication of Mary Lou's passion for raising horses. The bedroom wing is shown in the lower photograph, its windows covered with a louvered wood grille that shaded those inside from the sun. Although photographed while construction was nearing completion, these images provide an understanding of May's finishes for the home as well as the building's relationship to its prairie landscape. (Courtesy of the Frank Phillips Home.)

Kansas City, Missouri, architect David B. Runnells designed a one-story home for James and Elizabeth Akright in the Hillcrest Heights subdivision of Bartlesville in 1950. Runnells, a graduate of the Cranbrook Academy of Art in Bloomington Hills, Michigan, brought to Bartlesville a new type of modernism—one that was honed during his years working for Finnish-born architect Eliel Saarinen, Cranbrook's director. (Courtesy of Price Tower Arts Center Archives.)

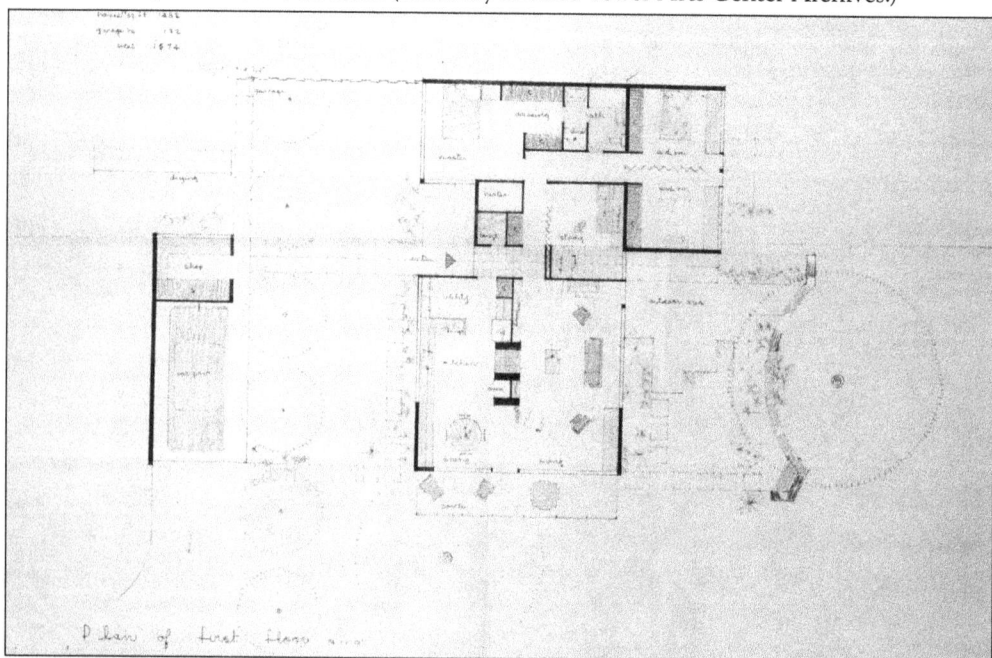

Runnells' plan was an assembly of box-shaped rooms on a four-foot grid, and included three bedrooms, study, and U-shaped kitchen, dining, and living area. The attached carport and workshop was connected to the main structure by a covered walkway and the home's bedrooms, kitchen, and living rooms featured adjacent patio spaces. (Courtesy of Price Tower Arts Center Archives.)

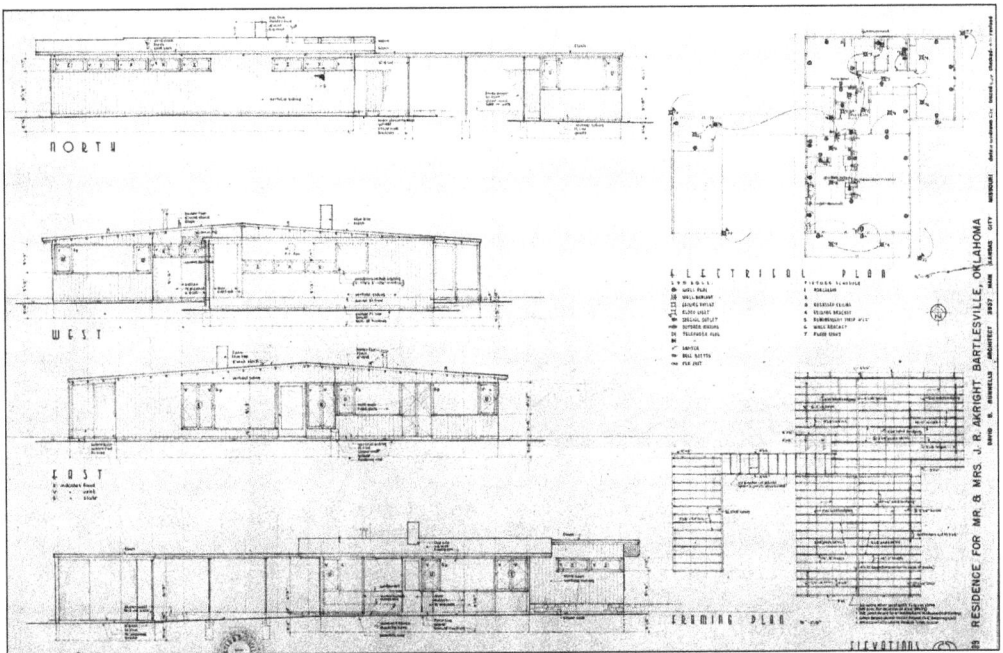

The elevation drawings (above) and section drawings (below) of the Akrights' home offer insight into Runnells's materiality and finish detailing. The home was sided vertically to visually heighten it, a subtle relief to the bands of awning windows, casement windows, and the rectilinear enclosed screen porch that enforced its horizontality. Inside the finishes included concrete floors, stone walls, and stained plywood with all storage and cabinetry constructed of stained plywood with sliding Masonite door panels. In keeping with the era's eschewal of decorative ornamental details, the graining of the plywood and the minimalist finger-hole openings of the Masonite door panels gave the interior an unpretentious air. (Above, courtesy of Price Tower Arts Center, 2007.22.05; below, courtesy of Price Tower Arts Center, 2007.22.06.)

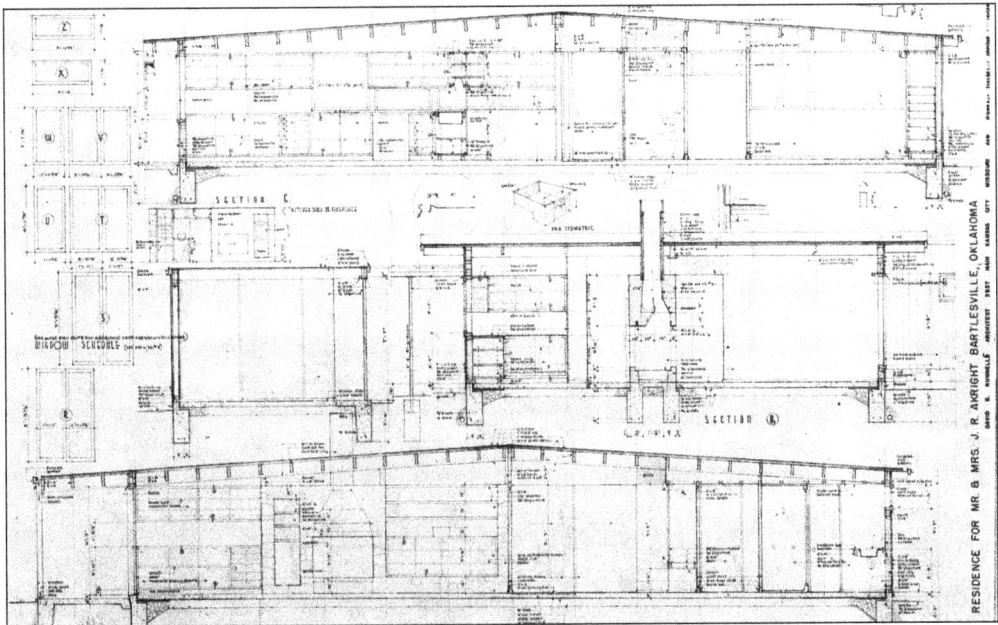

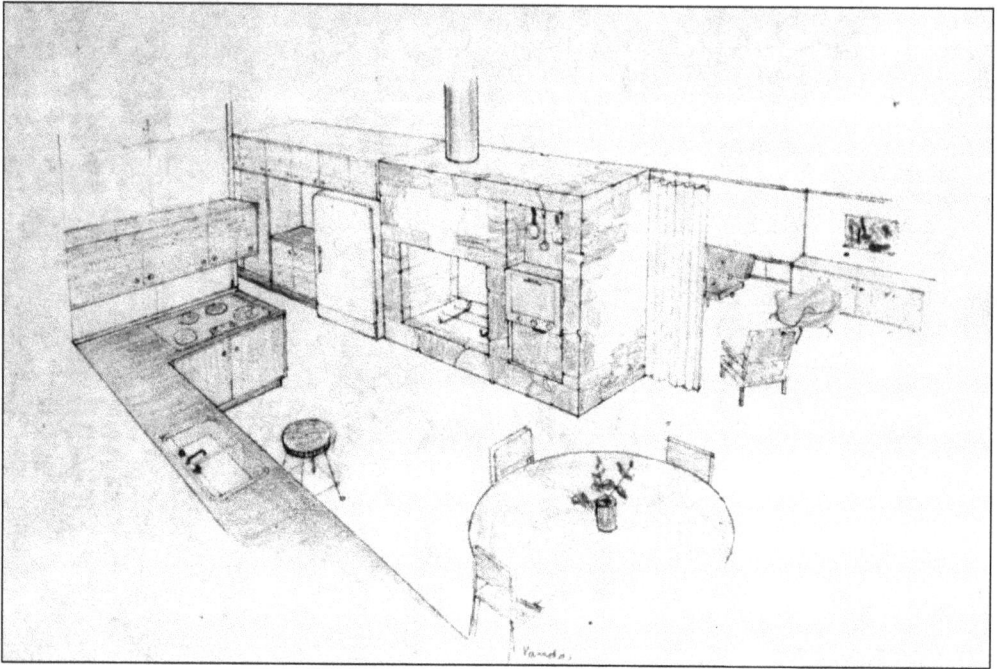

David Runnells's interior presentation drawings of the Akrights' kitchen, dining, and living areas shows the influences of his Cranbrook associations, especially in his choice of furniture, which are representations of many of his fellow classmates—Charles Eames, Ray Kaiser Eames, and Eero Saarinien among them. The sculptural aspect of these furnishings fit well into Runnells's open plan and also speaks well of the Akrights as mid-century consumers. Their appreciation of the good design lifestyle was one being exhibited at galleries and museums such as the Museum of Modern Art in New York City. (Courtesy of Price Tower Arts Center Archives.)

In 1959, the Akrights commissioned Bruce Goff to design an expansion to their home. Goff utilized the land between the house and the carport and created a high-ceilinged recreation room with a double-height stone fireplace set upon a triangular hearth. Goff turned Runnells' square grid on end, forming diamond shapes to create a new module for his addition. The screen porch was expanded, its framework a series of stacked diamond forms resting in a sawtooth-shaped foundation. The rear of the addition included a larger master bedroom suite that, along with the recreation room, looked out onto an outdoor patio with water pond and sitting area. (Above, courtesy of Price Tower Arts Center, 2007.22.12; below, courtesy of Price Tower Arts Center, 2007.22.13.)

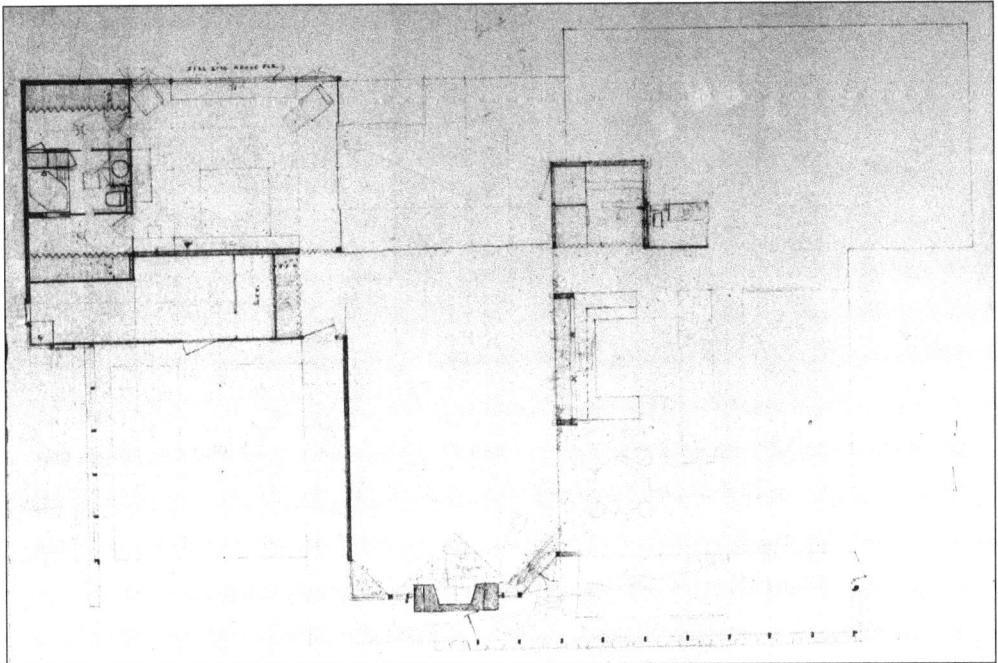

Joe Price, the youngest son of H. C. Price Company founders Mary Lou and Harold Price Sr., became the major patron of architect Bruce Goff, commissioning him three times to design his residence and its subsequent additions. Goff's unrealized bachelor studio for Price (around 1954), designed on the family's plot of farmland, was a floating faceted "pod" reached by an angular pathway. (Courtesy of Price Tower Arts Center, 2003.08.002.)

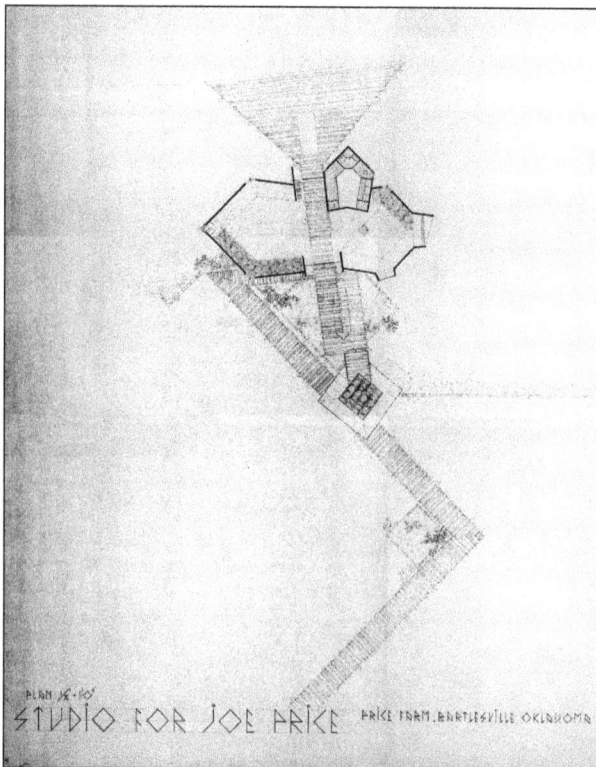

Joe Price's studio was comprised of three elongated pentagons, whose angled walls and sloping ceilings attached themselves to the intersecting wooden pathway like crystals. The studio's interior scheme included a fantastic use of materials—inlaid black linoleum flooring, white carpeting that extended up onto the purple-tinted mirrored walls, burnt cork paneling, and glass cullets imbedded into the exterior wall mortar. (Courtesy of Price Tower Arts Center, 2003.08.003.)

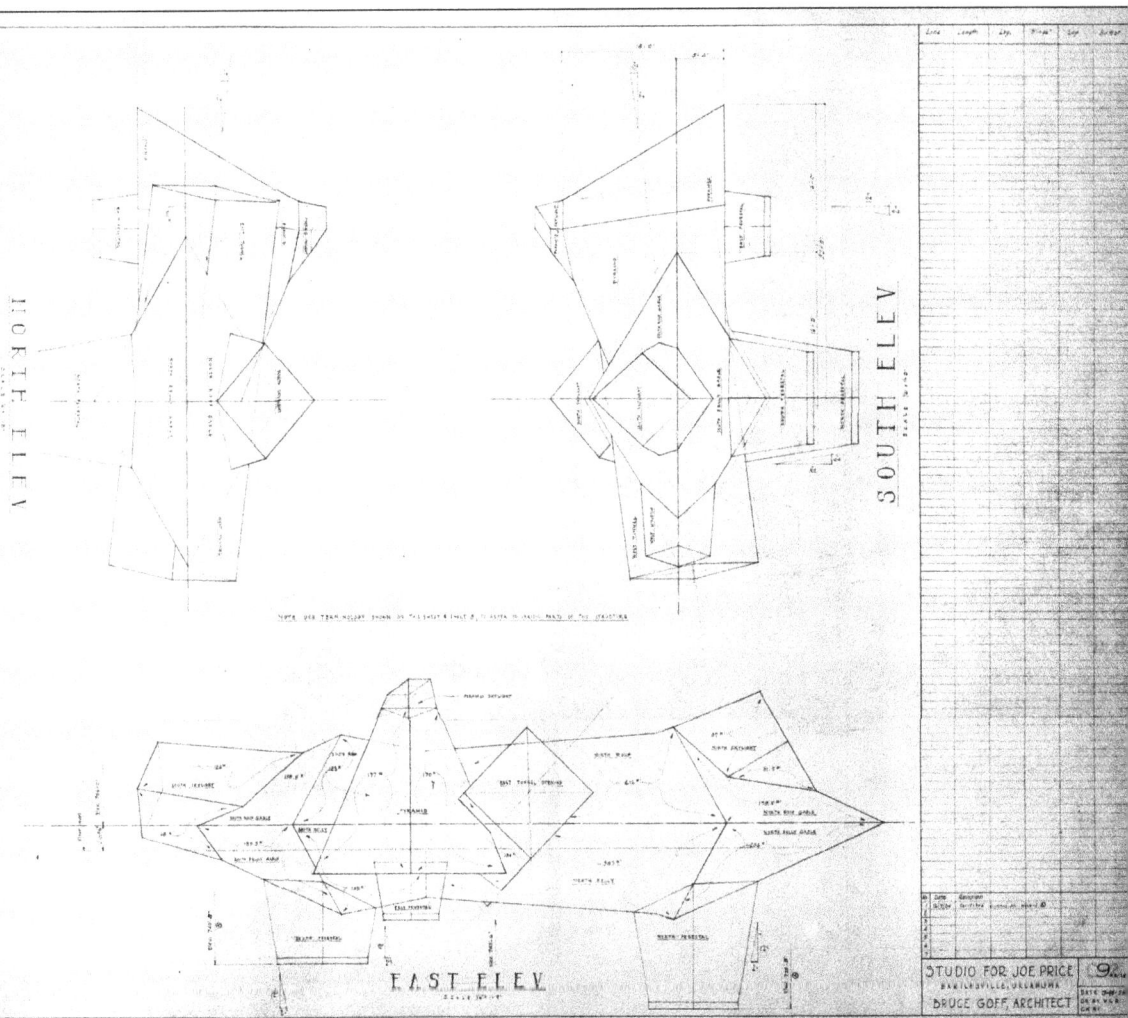

SOUTH ELEV

EAST ELEV

STUDIO FOR JOE PRICE
BARTLESVILLE, OKLAHOMA
BRUCE GOFF, ARCHITECT

The exterior details of Goff's studio plan for Price are shown on a multiview drawing from late 1954. The raised crystalline form, with its roots in post–World War I German architectural ideology, was not a practical one by any means. Resting on three large pedestals, the studio was a conglomeration of pyramidal and rectilinear forms, some of which were transparent to create skylight windows. The floor line bisected the studio lengthwise, and the construction framework was much like that of an airplane fuselage. Goff created names for the various "tunnels," "bellies," and "gables" of the structure and noted that all documents must refer to this idiosyncratic phraseology. The processional pathway leading across the property to the studio entrance purposefully meandered across the site, making right turns around planting boxes of fieldstone and glass cullets. (Courtesy of Price Tower Arts Center, 2003.08.112.)

Bruce Goff's second design for Joe Price was realized in 1958 and was very much different from the 1954 scheme. A more restrained angularity was employed, with an equilateral triangle being the primary geometric element. The studio's faceted form still floated upon stone piers, but the new angularity of the design's three wings visually continued the projection outward from the center of the plan. From the northeast, the studio's foundation walls, made of glass cullets and anthracite, are jagged, seemingly rising from the earth to support the architecture. They provide a textural contrast to the anodized aluminum cladding of the eastern wing, shown left, that glistened in the Oklahoma sun. The color palette of Goff's design—blue-green glass, gold aluminum, black anthracite with dark green mortar joints—was warm and rich and meant to convey a level of sophistication. (Courtesy of the Art Institute of Chicago.)

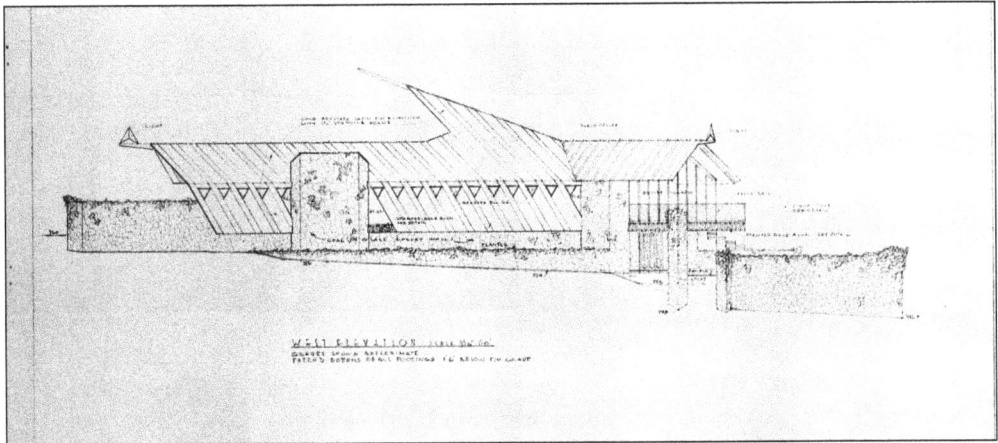

The aluminum-clad eastern wing featured a marching line of triangular portal windows, bringing light into the pyramidal interior and strengthening the geometric language of the overall design. Gold-painted pierced cast aluminum triangles, bronze screen window screens, and triangular finial lighting provided ornamental interest. (Courtesy of Price Tower Arts Center, 2003.08.051.)

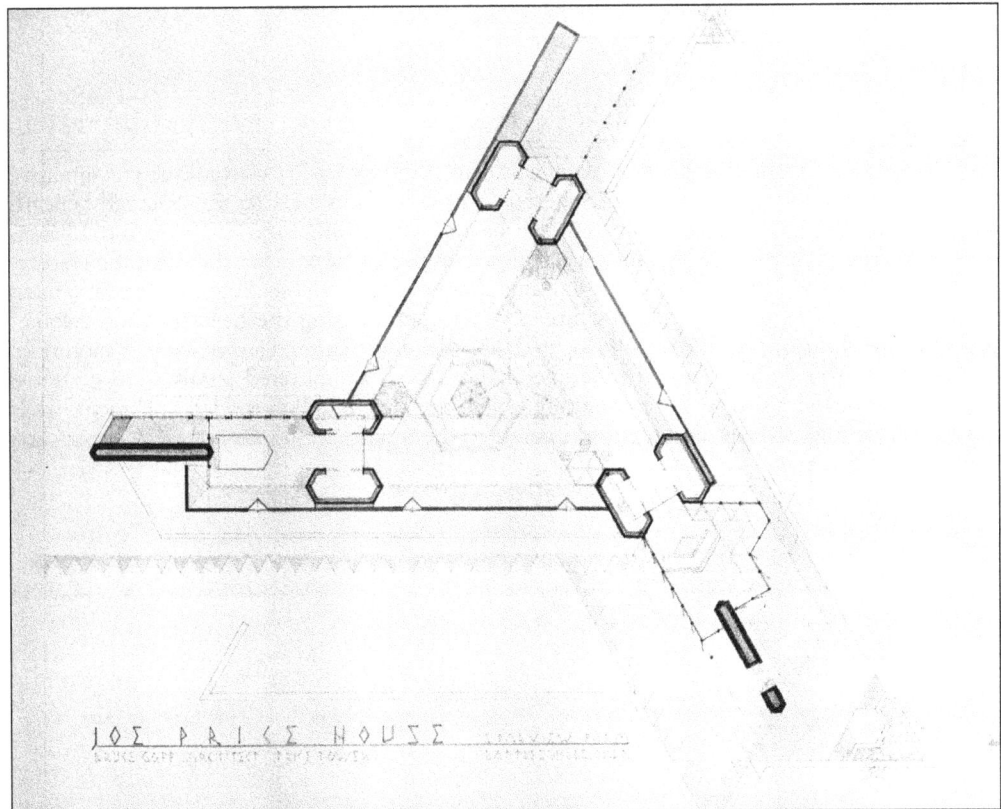

The c. 1956 plan of Joe Price's studio was based upon equilateral triangles and the hexagonal forms when they are combined. The three wings housed the bedroom, carport, and screened porch with closets, kitchen, and bathroom located within the hexagonal tips of the triangle. (Courtesy of Price Tower Arts Center, 2003.08.043.)

JOE PRICE STUDIO

Like the exterior, the interior scheme designed by Bruce Goff for Joe Price's studio was imaginative and resplendent in texture, color, and materials. The studio's living area was oriented beneath a pyramidal ceiling framed with black wooden beams. The ceiling surfaces between the beams were powdered with white goose down and cellophane strips hung from the central clerestory window to provide aural as well as visual amusement. The main seating area was a sunken "conversation pit" of heavily padded white carpeting, eliminating the need for "bothersome" portable furnishings, with its centrally located hexagonal wet bar and stereo cabinet motorized to lower into the floor. Along the perimeter, hexagonal upholstered stools were clustered around interior fountains and the structure's blue-green glass cullet-studded anthracite walls offered diffuse natural light and textural interest to the interior. (Courtesy of Price Tower Arts Center, 2003.08.042.)

The 1957 residence for real-estate and insurance agent C. A. Comer in Dewey is often included in Goff's Bartlesville work due to its proximity, seven miles to the north. The Comers' home was a study of floating planes, spires, and cantilevered beams. The tri-lobed floor plan was a core of kitchen and service needs—its form reflected in the three arms of the chimney's stack. The exterior of the home was clad in light-colored brick and its wooden beams and vertical siding stained a dark red color. The long, low-hung carport roof was suspended from steel cables attached to the cantilevered beams, seemingly floating over the front drive while also reinforcing the horizontal lines of the brickwork. (Above, courtesy of the Art Institute of Chicago; below, courtesy of Price Tower Arts Center Archives.)

Bruce Goff designed the J. O. Motsenbocker residence in 1957, and its clamshell-like plan was comprised of an arc of seven trapezoidal wedge shapes focused toward an enclosed garden at the home's rear. Its strict symmetry in plan was lessened by its dynamic elevations, including a zigzag-shaped roofline and diamond clerestory windows that followed the sweeping arc along the front. (Courtesy of Price Tower Arts Center, 2005.03.)

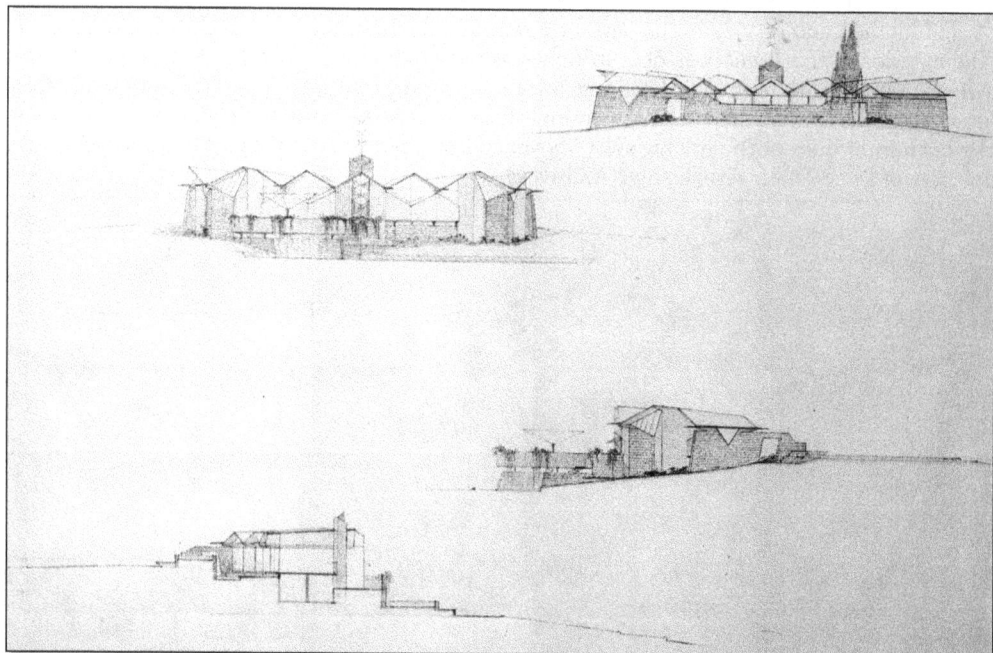

Atop a gentle sloping hill, the Motsenbocker residence's main floor, at street level, looked out upon a constructed landscape to the north from an arcing shingle-clad terrace. The exterior ornaments, including metal spires and notched cantilevered beams, were atop walls clad with light-colored masonry whose subtle board-and-batten-like texture captured light and shadows and strengthened the material's horizontality. (Courtesy of the Art Institute of Chicago.)

24

Howard Jones, a retired manufacturer of farm equipment, and his wife Lucile, commissioned Bruce Goff to design a home for them to retire to in 1958. The second of two plans for their Bartlesville residence, Goff utilized overlapping octagons for his two-story realized design, and its near-symmetrical plan was organized around a four-sided fireplace with hearths in the living, dining, kitchen, and hobby areas. Lower rooms could be closed off with wooden accordion partitions or left open for a circular flow. The upper floor, a semi-octagonal plan, housed the two bedrooms, their bathrooms, and a second-floor sundeck. The home's "birds mouth" windows allowed for the display of sculptural artwork along deep sills, and Goff's design for a site-specific custom braided wool rug for the interior reflected the Howards' interests in collecting early American glassware and furniture. Stained shingle siding and reddish-brown brick camouflaged the home within its tree-filled landscape. (Courtesy of the Art Institute of Chicago.)

Bruce Goff's 1959 rendering of the Richard and Joanne Bennett residence is representative of the architect's passion for Japanese paintings and prints. The asymmetrical framing was a technique used in the early work of Frank Lloyd Wright, whom Goff admired. The long pathways, square planting beds, and square slatted screens alluded to the home's interior floor plan grid and design elements. (Courtesy of Price Tower Arts Center, 2003.20.)

The L-shaped home's two-story living and cooking areas were positioned at the elbow, allowing for stacked fireplaces in the rear and a large diamond-shaped window in front, permitting an unobstructed view across the front yard and gardens, even while seated at the breakfast table. Stained wood shingles cover the exterior and slatted partitions support the covered walkways of each of the plan's extensions. (Courtesy of Price Tower Arts Center Archives.)

The James Fitchette residence, designed by Bruce Goff in 1961, was relatively reserved compared to Goff's earlier Bartlesville work. The strict rectilinear geometry of the plan was expressed vertically by tall plateglass windows and a wide chimney. Although the brick cladding provided horizontality to the design, it became an overall texture when applied to the home's massive structural walls. (Courtesy of the Art Institute of Chicago.)

Goff's cantilevered framework hovered above the eastern window, visually extending the skylight that ran laterally across the ceiling and divided the home's floor plan into distinct functional areas for sleeping, dining, and entertaining. The alabaster-like Kalwall material diffused natural light through the opening, which was supplemented by fluorescent perimeter lighting when needed. (Courtesy of Price Tower Arts Center Archives.)

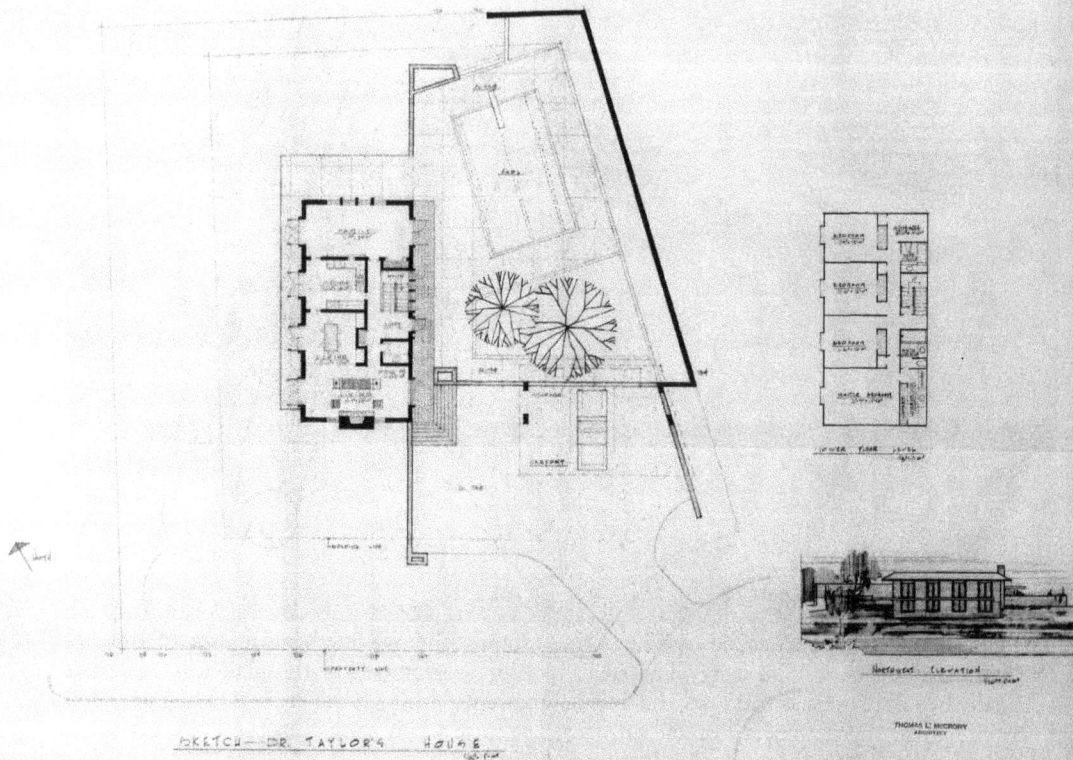

Bartlesville-based architect Thomas McCrory had a flourishing practice in the area following World War II, and his sketch design for the James and Nancy Taylor residence illustrated a creative solution for an oddly-shaped lot. The home, a compacted two-story structure, was arranged with the family's bedrooms on the lower level and kitchen, dining, living, and family rooms on the upper floor. The northwest elevation featured a terrace accessible from each of the public spaces, connecting to the pool patio and carport on the opposite side. The in-ground swimming pool, nearly the same dimensions as the home's footprint, is set at an angle parallel to the eastern property line. The hard-edged modernism of the Taylor design was a reaction to open plan types of residential architecture with McCrory offering a more compartmentalized scheme, enclosing each of the home's functions into specific rooms. (Courtesy of Ambler Architects.)

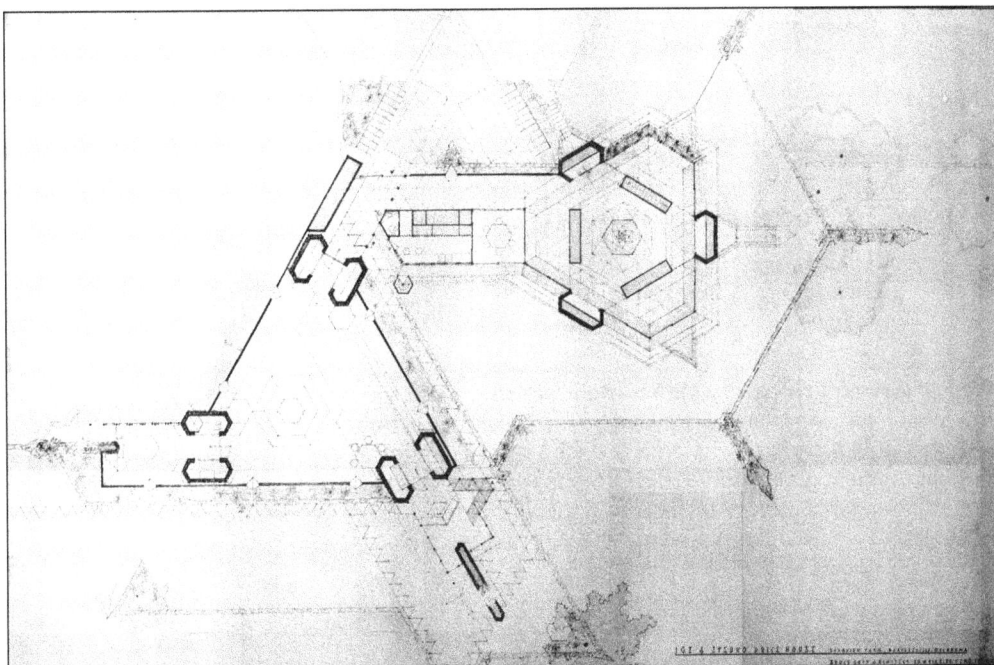

Two years after Joe Price's marriage to Etsuko Yoshimochi in 1964, Bruce Goff was commissioned to enlarge the bachelor's studio he designed nearly a decade earlier. A second triangular gallery wing was added and at the center of the addition's hexagonal sunken seating area was a star-shaped pool, itself forming the dramatic transparent faceted skylight of the sunken Japanese bath one level below. (Courtesy of Price Tower Arts Center, 2003.08.069.)

The exterior southwest elevation shows Goff's innovative use of materials, especially the foundation of anthracite and glass cullets. A by-product of glass manufacturing, the cullets permitted light to pass though them while maintaining privacy. The striking combination of dark and light colors, opaque and translucent light qualities, and jagged and smooth textures are expressive of Goff's modernity in using nontraditional building materials. (Courtesy of Price Tower Arts Center, 2003.08.065.)

This elevation of the new addition (right of center) and the carport (right) also illustrates the power of Goff's placement of the residence on its site. Seeming to rise out of the earth, anthracite and glass cullets form the base for terraced gardens and walking paths, the corners mounded with blue-green glass giving them the appearance of frozen icecaps on an extraterrestrial mountainscape. (Courtesy of Price Tower Arts Center, 2003.08.066.)

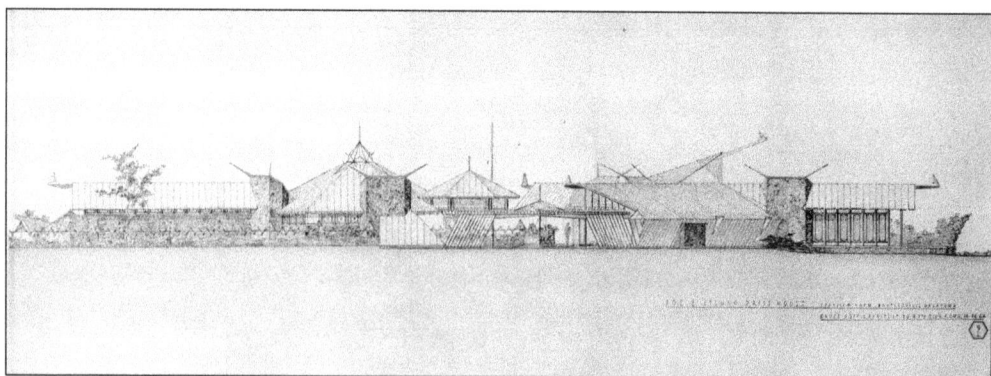

The roofline of the Price residence, although faceted, is dynamic and reinforces the horizontality of the building and its connection with the Oklahoma prairie landscape. Roofing beams project outward, continuing the line and terminating in modern triangular lighting elements. Recalling traditional Japanese temple construction details, the Price residence was designed, in part, to showcase the growing Japanese art collection of its patrons. (Courtesy of Price Tower Arts Center, 2003.08.067.)

30

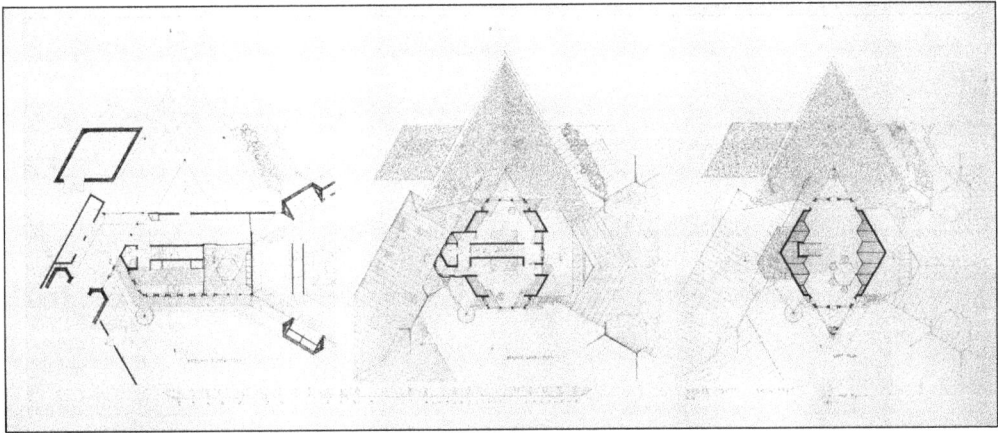

A second addition by Bruce Goff to the Joe and Etsuko Price residence in 1974 was a diamond-shaped "tower" that housed bedrooms and a hexagonal private study. It rose above the existing structure, and was capped with cantilevered triangular balconies and covered with the same gold-anodized aluminum roofing material as the rest of the structure. (Courtesy of Price Tower Arts Center, 2003.08.075.)

The section drawings by Goff illustrate the interior of Joe Price's "roost" atop the home. Designed to be a private studio for Price, it offered panoramic views from two balconies, and picturesque art-glass windows and doors, mirrored ceiling, and an abundance of cream-colored marble. (Courtesy of Price Tower Arts Center, 2003.08.080.)

The full-length east elevation (above) and west elevation (below) of the Price residence show the third floor roost as it was installed above the center of the three arms of the floor plan. Bruce Goff thus gave his client unobstructed views from both elevations of the anthracite and glass landscape below. The home's many projecting finials, perhaps inspired by architectural features seen by Goff and the Prices on their numerous trips to Southeast Asia and Japan, were either narrow and long or terminated in a triangular lighting element, which at night appeared to frame the home with dots of light. (Above, courtesy of Price Tower Arts Center, 2003.08.076; below, courtesy of Price Tower Arts Center, 2003.08.078.)

The full-length north elevation (above) and south elevation (below) of the Price residence illustrate the gold-colored anodized aluminum roof of each section of the home, each folded in an origami-like fashion that occasionally wrapped around the underside of the structure. The foundation and garden gates, constructed of lanolin-coated anthracite and glass fragments, were primitive looking, their hand-stacked appearance in juxtaposition to the machine-made smoothness of the aluminum cladding. From these vantage points, the home appeared to be a floating palace gliding along a black ocean of anthracite waves capped in blue-green glass cullets. (Above, courtesy of Price Tower Arts Center, 2003.08.079; below, courtesy of Price Tower Arts Center, 2003.08.077.)

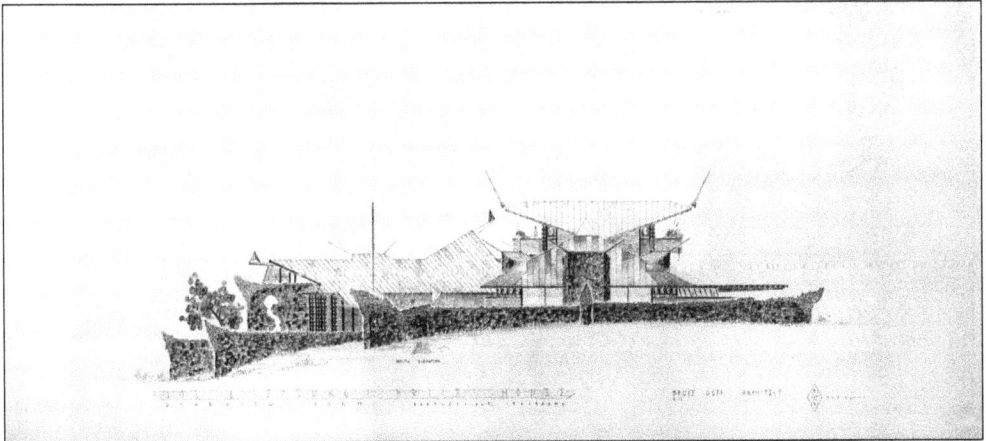

The Prices renamed their home Shin'enKan (a Chinese phrase meaning "house of the faraway heart") and opened it to nearly 4,000 visitors per year. Tours were conducted of the estate as well as of their growing collection of Japanese paintings and prints. Bruce Goff's most luxurious residential design, it became a conference center for the University of Oklahoma College of Architecture in 1985 when the Prices moved their family and art collection to southern California. In homage to Goff, who had died in 1982, Joe Price donated the home with the intention that it became a center dedicated to creative thinking. In 1996, the home was destroyed by fire, leaving few architectural and ornamental features to survive. Seen are, from left to right, Jill Trolinger, Alex Yorman, Teresa Carrig, and Jane Waters visiting during a YWCA adult education tour in April 1987. (Courtesy of the Bartlesville Area History Museum.)

The Ambler residence, designed by architect and Bartlesville native Scott Ambler for his family, was completed in 1998 in the city's Stonebridge subdivision. As inspiration, Scott and Martha Ambler looked to the classic Italian villa, a casual architectural style in which history is everywhere apparent, yet they incorporated modern features into the two-story, 3,800-square-foot home. No part of the home's T-shaped floor plan is ever more than 19 feet wide, and an abundance of natural light is due in large part to the quantity of windows (52) a feature Ambler noted gave them "one to clean each week." (Courtesy of Ambler Architects.)

The rear of the Ambler residence was symmetrically designed to feature a pair of wide covered porches flanking the arched window of the breakfast nook and centered beneath a marching row of 10 windows that drew light into the second-floor interior. The swimming pool, aligned to create a secondary axis through the home's plan, and surrounding gardens provide an outdoor entertaining area that recalls the Amblers' Italianate inspiration. A series of four architectural columns, rescued from downtown Bartlesville buildings slated for demolition or renovation, offer an additional historical backdrop while also representing the owners' love of architecture. (Courtesy of Ambler Architects.)

Two

A HILLSIDE HOME, A TREE, AND A SHELL

FRANK LLOYD WRIGHT AND TALIESIN IN BARTLESVILLE

The three projects in this chapter are inextricably linked in spirit and philosophy. The residence for Carolyn and Harold Price Jr. was designed by Frank Lloyd Wright in 1954 at the same time as Price's father's company was constructing a 19-story corporate headquarters in downtown Bartlesville. Price Tower, home of the H. C. Price Company, was completed in 1956 and among Wright's last public commissions. As his only realized skyscraper, Price Tower is a masterpiece of experimental construction techniques and made of materials not typically thought of in the canon of mid-20th-century high-rise architecture.

The Bartlesville Community Center, which opened in 1982, was designed by William Wesley Peters, Wright's former son-in-law and an early apprentice who was charged with running the Taliesin firm following the master's death in 1959. Twenty years later, as his design grew from the city block opposite Price Tower, it became apparent that the geometric language and organic relationships professed by Wright had indeed carried over to the next generation of Taliesin architects.

Each project was different in function—a residential home for a large family, a multiuse high-rise tower, and a public community center designed for multiple user groups, yet they share several overlapping architectural principles and similar materials. The influence of geometry—rectangles and squares for the Price residence, triangles and parallelograms for Price Tower, and circles and ovals for the community center—was integral to Wrightian architecture, a principle continued by Taliesin. Organic relationships to the landscape and nature were also important considerations in each design, whether seeming to project from it, or be constructed of the stone, trees, and metals comprising it.

Wright's Bartlesville architecture was designed for a private and corporate client while Taliesin's was for the public overall, and this is perhaps the most interesting aspect of the trio. Rarely has a body of architectural principles applied so successfully to such varied types of buildings, and along with those works by Bruce Goff, make Bartlesville a true distinctive destination for modern American architecture.

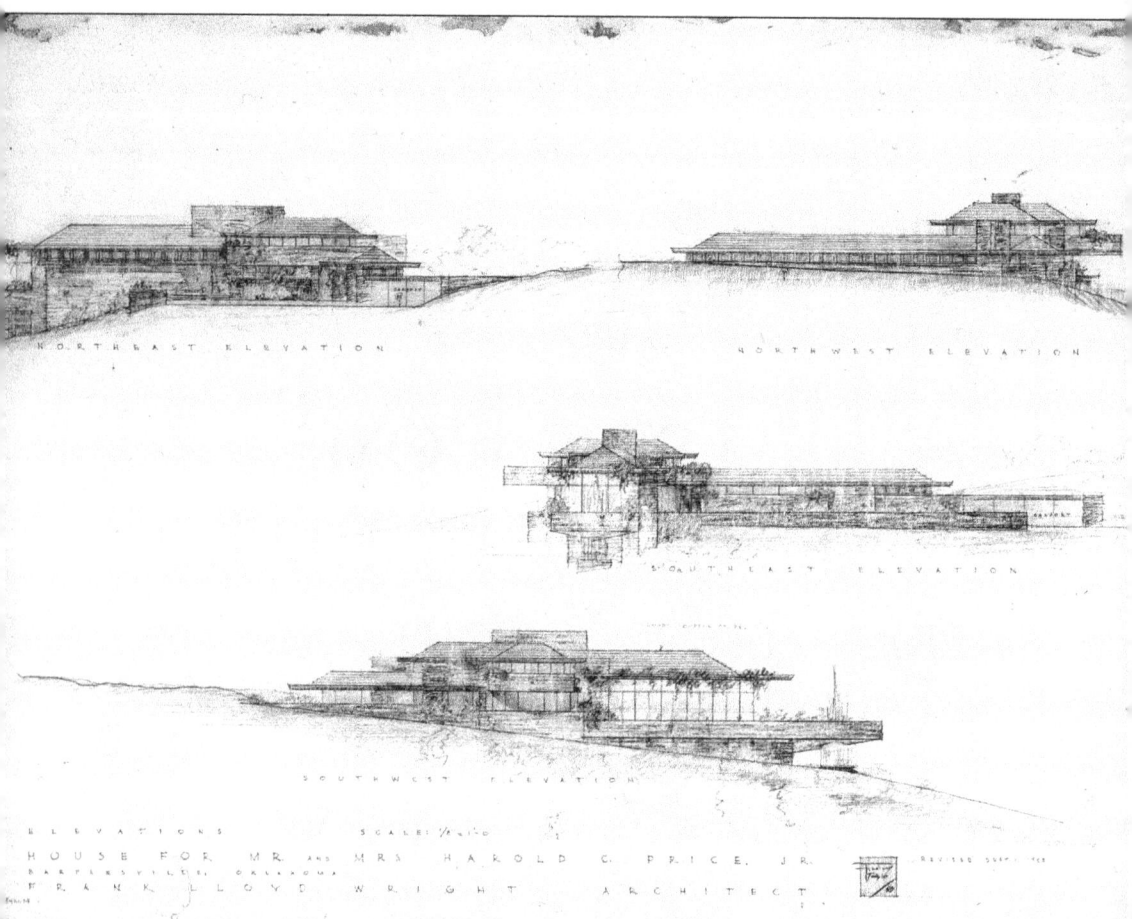

NORTHEAST ELEVATION

NORTHWEST ELEVATION

SOUTHEAST ELEVATION

SOUTHWEST ELEVATION

ELEVATIONS   SCALE: 1/8"=1'-0"
HOUSE FOR MR. AND MRS. HAROLD C. PRICE. JR.
BARTLESVILLE, OKLAHOMA
FRANK LLOYD WRIGHT   ARCHITECT

In 1954, Harold Price Jr. and his wife, Carolyn, commissioned Frank Lloyd Wright to design a home for their family—soon to include six children—on the Price family's Star View Farm property. A long, horizontal structure, similar in many ways to Wright's early prairie estates, Hillside, as it became known, was designed as if evolving from the land rather than built upon it. The deep eaves, low roofline, and extended terrace increased the sense of horizontality and unified the structure with its surroundings. The cantilevered construction techniques used by Wright were personified in earlier projects, such as his famed 1935 Fallingwater home for the Kaufmann family near Bear Run, Pennsylvania, and even in the designs for the Price Tower, which was under construction at the same time. (Copyright 1988, the Frank Lloyd Wright Foundation, Taliesin West, Scottsdale, Arizona, 5421.004.)

As realized, the Prices' Hillside residence was an L-shaped plan with one arm terminating in a carport and the other in a double-height living area with large terrace. Its brick and wood exterior drew upon Frank Lloyd Wright's fondness for organic materials, as did its abundance of windows, which brought in natural daylight and fresh air but also served to link the exterior with an interior that shared the same palette of materials. From the southeast, above, the horizontality of the home in relation to its landscape and the dramatic cantilever of the terrace can be seen while from the southwest, below, the impact of the living area's tall windows becomes apparent and a second cantilevered terrace continues Wright's play between solid and void. (Above, copyright Maynard Parker, the Frank Lloyd Wright Foundation, Taliesin West, Scottsdale, Arizona, 5421.0018; below, copyright Maynard Parker, the Frank Lloyd Wright Foundation, Taliesin West, Scottsdale, Arizona, 5421.0023.)

Two opposing views of Hillside's double-height living area exemplify the spatial techniques employed by Frank Lloyd Wright in many of his residential projects. The wooden strips decorating the hipped roof force the viewer's eye upward, making the ceiling feel taller while the narrow Roman brick draws the eye lengthwise, adding to the interior's horizontality. The room's eastern wall featured a built-in easel for displaying the couple's collection of paintings and works on paper and other built-in elements included a banquette sofa next to the fireplace and an abundance of wall shelving. The moveable furniture was a mix of the Prices' own selections and those designed by Wright, especially the cluster of triangular and hexagonal occasional tables designed for Heritage-Henredon in 1955. (Above, copyright Maynard Parker, the Frank Lloyd Wright Foundation, Taliesin West, Scottsdale, Arizona, 5421.0011; below, copyright Maynard Parker, the Frank Lloyd Wright Foundation, Taliesin West, Scottsdale, Arizona, 5421.0018.)

A scale model of the Price Tower was constructed for the Price family by Frank Lloyd Wright's apprentices at his Taliesin Fellowship in Spring Green, Wisconsin, soon following the approval of the plans. The model made its debut during the International Petroleum Exposition in Tulsa from May 14–23, 1953. An opportunity to present the design for the H. C. Price Company's new building to the oil company executives who were its clients, the event drew approximately 250,000 visitors and was attended by Wright as well, helping Price to promote what would become, three years later, the architect's first realized skyscraper. In this photograph, the entire Price family—from left to right Joe, Mary Lou, Harold Sr., and Harold Jr.—was present and proudly posed in front of the model as it was displayed in the exposition's Oklahoma Building. (Courtesy of Price Tower Arts Center Archives.)

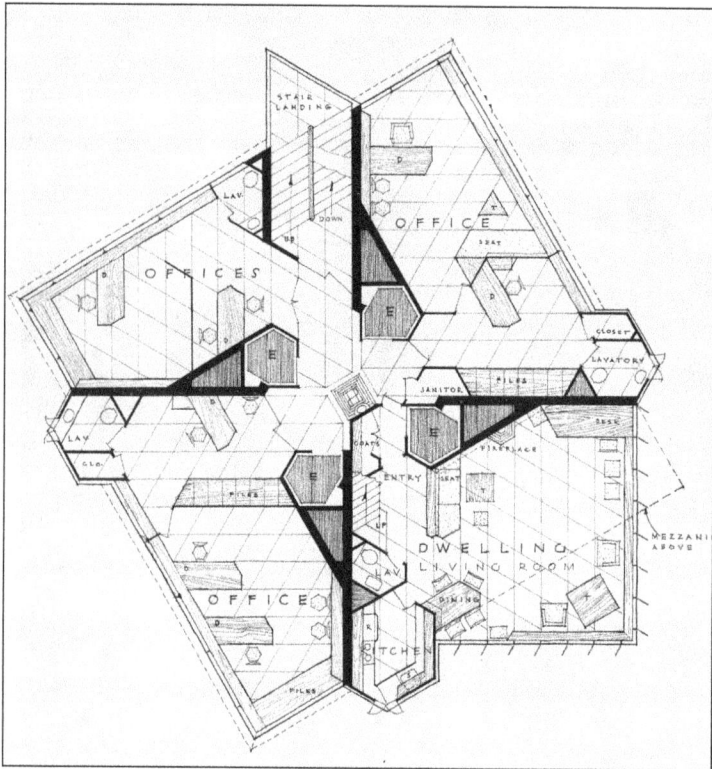

The plans of a typical floor and bedroom mezzanine of the Price Tower featured a diamond-shaped grid incised into the pigmented concrete floors that regulated the location of walls, built-in furniture, and even the shape of the elevators, and an inlaid bronze medallion incorporating the H. C. Price Company logo: HCPCo. Pinwheel-shaped structural walls terminated in elevator shafts, with each apartments' located within the unit to provide occupants with private access from the first floor. (Courtesy of Price Tower Arts Center Archives.)

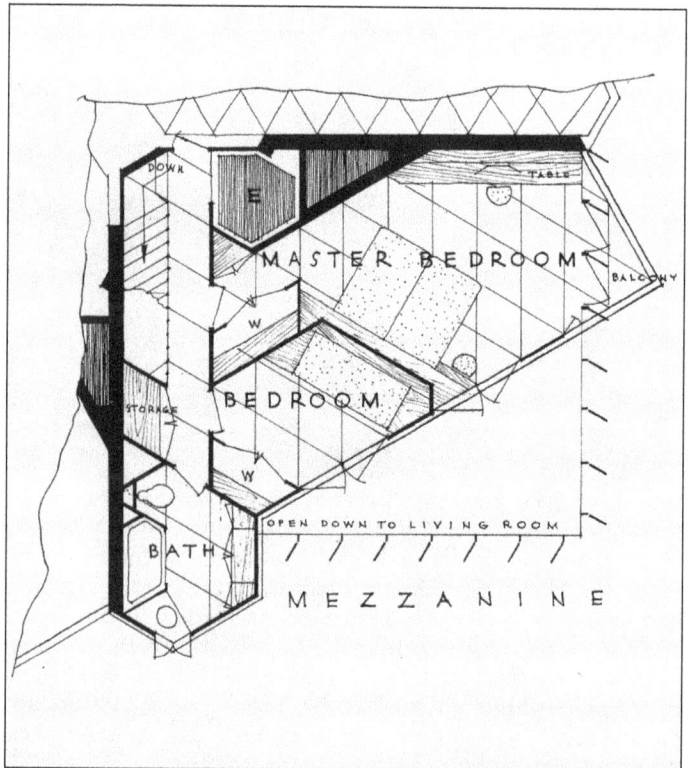

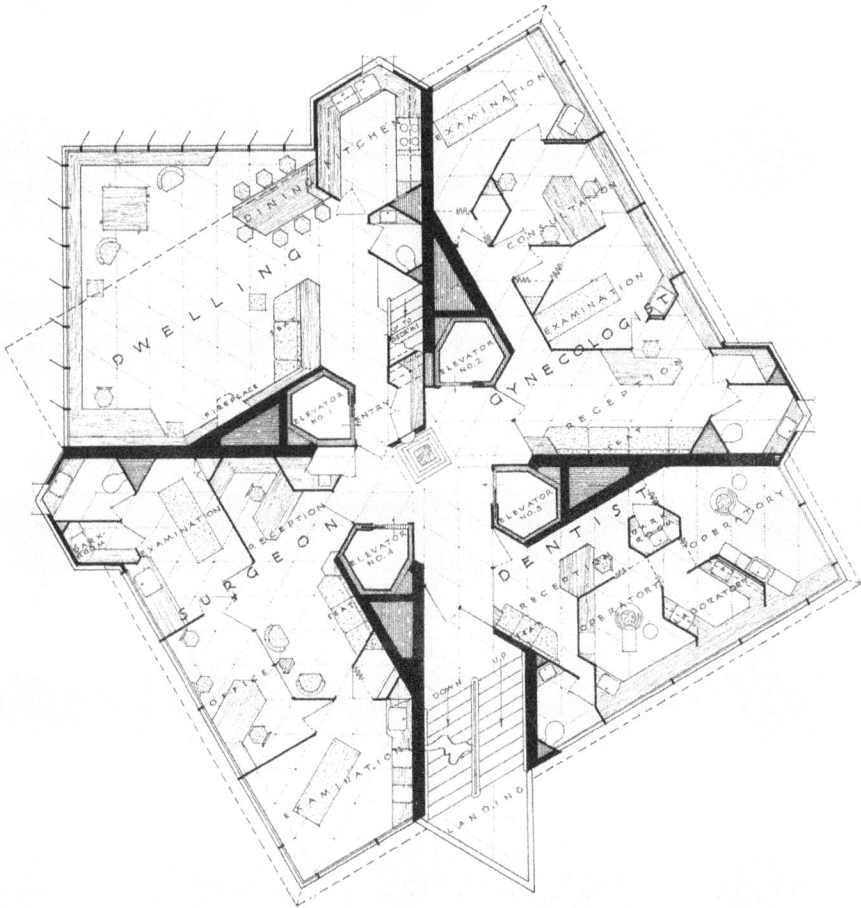

The plan of a typical floor of Price Tower, taken from the 1956 opening weekend press packet, shows suggestions for tenants—surgeon, gynecologist, dentist, and apartment dweller—and the possibilities for individualized room arrangements within the Frank Lloyd Wright–designed structure. These ideal tenants were undoubtedly the sort Price (and Wright) hoped to secure, as they would have the means and cultural savvy to understand the importance of the building. The leasing of the offices and apartments was handled by the Price Company and while offices were considered prime real estate, the apartments did not rent and were eventually adapted to meet the demand of office tenants. Private offices each had a lavatory and coat closet and were designed to efficiently hold two to four work stations; larger firms would rent multiple offices or entire floors, often using the triangular exterior staircase to travel between floors. (Courtesy of Price Tower Arts Center, 2004.12.1-i.)

The site of the headquarters for the H. C. Price Company was located on two city lots near the intersection of Dewey Avenue and Sixth Street (now Silas Street), one block south and the opposite side of Dewey Avenue than had been first selected by Harold Price Sr., Frank Lloyd Wright was able to convince his client that a great building should cast its own shadow upon its own land, and not be threatened by encroaching structures or be in competition with other tall buildings. The Price Company eventually purchased the entire city block and removed all small structures except for an automobile dealership, seen on the left of these two images. (Above, courtesy of Price Tower Arts Center, 2003.16.001; below, courtesy of Price Tower Arts Center, 2003.16.002.)

The building committee overseeing the Price Tower project was comprised of members of the Price family. Mary Lou Patteson Price and Harold Charles Price Sr., on the left, visited Frank Lloyd Wright at his Wisconsin home, Taliesin, flying there on the Price Company airplane. Harold Jr., right, and his brother Joe, who captured this moment on film, assisted with the supervision on the job site. Joe Price's photographs and film footage of the Price Tower document the building process from ground-breaking to public opening, and span nearly four years. The Prices commissioned Wright for three projects including the Paradise Valley, Arizona, residence for Harold Sr. and Mary Lou (known as the Grandma House) and a Bartlesville residence, known as Hillside, for Harold Jr., his wife Carolyn Propps Price, and their six children. Joe Price was the patron of architect Bruce Goff, commissioning him for Bartlesville and Lake Tahoe residences, and for the location of his Japanese art collection, known as Shin'enKan. (Courtesy of Price Tower Arts Center, 2003.16.003.)

The construction of the Price Company's headquarters was an attraction in itself. The model of the building debuted at the Tulsa oil exposition in 1952, and once digging for the foundation began, tourists and curious local townsfolk often stopped to watch the action. (Courtesy of Price Tower Arts Center, 2003.16.006.)

Once the foundation framing was completed, the pouring of liquid cement began. Wright's modified "tap root" foundation served to strengthen the Price Tower much like the tap roots of the tree—allowing for the weight of the tall building to rest upon a central core rather than needing outer structural walls. (Courtesy of Price Tower Arts Center, 2003.16.009.)

Although not visible from the exterior, one of the Price Tower's major construction materials was steel—utilized as reinforcing elements for the cantilevered concrete structure. The combinations of straight, curved, and meshed reinforcing rods gave the 19-story skyscraper its rigidity and the support necessary to carry the load of its upper floors, their contents, and occupants as well as withstand the strong winds and storms that frequently befall Oklahoma. The narrow diameter of the reinforcing rods allowed for floors and ceilings that tapered outward toward the edges of the building giving the resulting form a sculptured quality. (Right, courtesy of Price Tower Arts Center, 2003.16.138; below, courtesy of Price Tower Arts Center, 2003.16.139.)

Joe Price's photographic study of the building of the Price Tower for his father's company often ventured toward the artistic in its formal appreciation of texture, lighting qualities, and material. An array of newly delivered bundled steel reinforcing bars (left) laid out along the ground at the construction site becomes an expressionistic composition of light and shadow. Stacked plywood forms, below, used to create the larger expanses of reinforced concrete wall surfaces, have a quiltlike appearance when assembled, the subtly of their grid work apparent on the finished surfaces of the hardened concrete. (Left, courtesy of Price Tower Arts Center, 2003.16.129; below, courtesy of Price Tower Arts Center, 2003.16.179.)

From the ground floor on up, the methods of creating walls and floors remained the same. Construction crews placed steel reinforcing bars and reinforcing mesh into place then assembled the plywood framing. Concrete was poured between the plywood walls, surrounding the reinforcing bars and locking them into place during the curing process. (Courtesy of Price Tower Arts Center, 2003.16.011.)

Frank Lloyd Wright's use of concrete as a material for the Price Tower allowed for dramatic cantilevers, such as these near the building's entrance. Because the structural supports were located at the center of the floor plan, there was no need for outside supports, and large plates of glass could then meet at corners without the visual distraction of a support member. (Courtesy of Price Tower Arts Center, 2003.16.012.)

A two-story base was designed by Wright for leased tenant spaces and a street-level caretaker's apartment. The roof of the wing, originally including a rooftop garden and fountain, was altered to accommodate a large skylight that flooded the double-height interiors below with natural light. To the right, an open air perforated concrete wall served as a screen for the building's air conditioning units. (Courtesy of Price Tower Arts Center, 2003.16.018.)

Atop the two-story wing, 14 smaller floors continued above, and their plan was consistent: a double-height apartment in the southwest quadrant, and a private office in each remaining quadrant. Each floor took approximately three weeks to cure before the next could be added. (Courtesy of Price Tower Arts Center, 2003.16.029.)

These views, both taken from the southwest, show construction as the Price Tower reaches the fifth floor (right) and ninth floor (below). The pinwheel-like geometry of Wright's floor plan becomes more apparent, and the cantilevered corners of each story ever more dramatic. The wooden supports used to hold the plywood concrete forms in place move up the building, following construction as each story is completed. Since elevators were not yet installed, and the exterior staircase was concrete and formed floor-by-floor, much of the transportation of materials and workers by construction crews was via temporary scaffolding stairs and elevators. (Right, courtesy of Price Tower Arts Center, 2003.16.034; below, courtesy of Price Tower Arts Center, 2003.16.046.)

51

The exterior of the Price Tower also featured horizontal bands of copper tiles, large embossed panels of copper sheeting that were inserted into the plywood framing before the concrete was poured, locking them into place as the concrete hardened. The copper panels were placed only on the exteriors of the even-numbered floors, creating a ribbon that wraps around the tower and bends inward to cover the face of each apartment's bedroom loft parapet. This contrivance also exemplified Wright's philosophy of organic architecture by bringing a bit of the building's exterior into the interior decoration, a relationship he also utilized in his design of furnishings. In the foreground, a covered walkway linked the caretaker's apartment to the residential carport and allowed for additional rooftop garden areas. The vertical perforations of the air conditioning room provide ventilation and were a curious foil to the otherwise horizontal bands of windows elsewhere in the tower. (Courtesy of Price Tower Arts Center, 2003.16.047.)

Frank Lloyd Wright's design for the embossed copper panels is derived from earlier conceptual designs for the St. Mark's-in-the-Bouwerie towers and is an amalgamation of triangles, double parallelograms, and rectangles. The panels, shown at right, were preformed and designed to interlock together during the concrete's curing process. To keep the pattern from flattening or bending out of shape, the plywood forms, shown below, were designed to reinforce the embossed ornamentation. A mirror image of the panels themselves, the plywood was attached to the outside surface of the copper panels and kept the entire unit rigid. (Right, courtesy of Price Tower Arts Center, 2003.16.120; below, courtesy of Price Tower Arts Center, 2003.16.122.)

Construction workers place a stretch of the copper panels (shown in reverse) into the protective plywood framing, resting it on a ledge that keeps the panels level while the concrete hardens. While the copper sheet made the panels lightweight and easy to emboss, it also made them susceptible to damage if mishandled. (Courtesy of Price Tower Arts Center, 2003.16.157.)

Once the concrete had cured, the exterior protective plywood could be removed, revealing the embossed copper surface beneath. While Frank Lloyd Wright knew the properties of copper would cause the panels to patinate over time, he preferred the green appearance and the building's copper details, including the louvers and spire, were patinated by hand. (Courtesy of Price Tower Arts Center, 2003.16.156.)

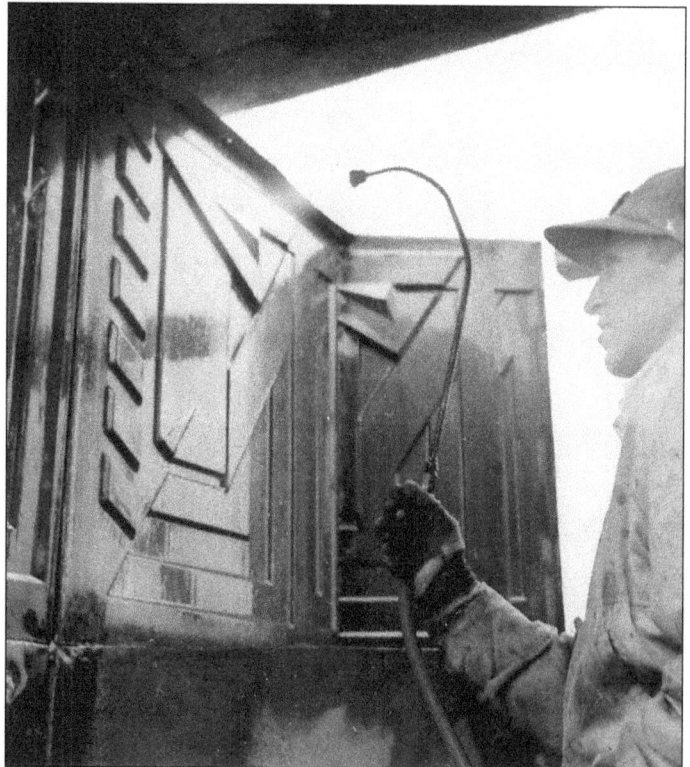

The patination of the Price Tower's exterior embossed copper panels was laborious and especially difficult on the upper floors. A chemically-induced process, and one that no doubt utilized the H. C. Price Company's expertise in chemical coatings, each panel was sprayed and then wiped down after a specified time in order to halt the process. The exact chemical product is unknown, although it was often mythologized as having been horse urine. Wright's ideal finish, dark teal-green in nature, still allowed for some variation, and the streaking and dripping of the chemical added to the visual texture of the panels from a distance. (Right, courtesy of Price Tower Arts Center, 2003.16.158; below, courtesy of Price Tower Arts Center, 2003.16.160.)

The southwestern elevation, including the quadrant of double-height apartments, was an animated arrangement of the projecting corners of each apartment's living and dining areas and the flat parapet of the bedroom loft. Once the windows were in place, this alternation became less apparent and is best viewed from the apartments' interiors or when the apartments are lit at night. (Courtesy of Price Tower Arts Center, 2003.16.087.)

An efficiency-style kitchen on the lower level of each double-height apartment was stacked with a bathroom above it, to service the bedroom loft. This kitchen-bathroom arrangement is made apparent on the tower's exterior as a vertical column along the western elevation. Those projections aligning with the bands of unadorned concrete were kitchens; those adjacent to the bands of copper panels were bathrooms. (Courtesy of Price Tower Arts Center, 2003.16.094.)

By November 1954, one year after the groundbreaking, construction reached the 14th floor and the Price Tower's verticality seemed unending. Without their windows in place, the cantilevered floors appear as stacked plates or haphazardly arranged books. The sawtooth-like triangular staircase, shown at right in the lower image, marches vertically along the eastern elevation and creates a spine to the tower. Each level of the staircase tapers slightly upward at its point, giving one the feeling of standing at a ship's prow; at night, its lights provide a dotted line upward toward the roof, and is continued by the lights of the tower's copper spire. (Right, courtesy of Price Tower Arts Center, 2003.16.056; below, courtesy of Price Tower Arts Center, 2003.16.059.)

In two photographs taken from the tower of the downtown fire station two blocks away, the Price Tower's visual impact upon the skyline of Bartlesville is ever apparent. Frank Lloyd Wright's tower, earning its nicknamed "the tree that escaped the crowded forest," truly stands out among the one- and two-story structures that comprised most of the city's downtown. The meaning behind the nickname was two-fold, alluding to its predecessor and to its method of construction—Wright's 1927 design for a New York City apartment tower, St. Marks-in-the-Bouwerie, realized in his multiuse Price Tower, figuratively escaped from the crowded forest of Manhattan skyscrapers and its cantilevered construction with a "trunk" of elevator shafts balancing the "branches" of tapering floors and ceilings covered in "leaves" of patinated copper tiles made either anecdote perfectly acceptable. (Left, courtesy of Price Tower Arts Center, 2003.063; below, courtesy of Price Tower Arts Center, 2003.068.)

As the Price Tower construction reaches the upper floors, a shift in the design occurs. The floor plan becomes more compact, and concentrates on the southeast quadrant. At the 15th floor, the three quadrants of office spaces are topped off with a concrete roof, allowing for large rooftop dining terraces on the 16th floor. These terraces, along with a small luncheon counter, constituted the private commissary for the H. C. Price Company employees, who often enjoyed their lunch alfresco high atop the Price Tower. From afar, the vertical concrete structural walls, hidden within the structure on the lower floors, rise out of the center of the building and create a spectacular crown to the skyscraper. (Right, courtesy of Price Tower Arts Center, 2003.16.073; below, courtesy of Price Tower Arts Center, 2003.16.077.)

Joe Price photographed the building each step of the way and served as the de facto documentalist for the Price Tower commission. Even the seemingly mundane images of the Price Tower—here two photographs show the aluminum brackets attached to the apartment quadrant, awaiting their vertical patinated copper louvers—were given thoughtful consideration. The Price Tower's manufactured components, such as the cast aluminum window brackets, were specially designed and were interesting as objects in their own right; en masse, and without their louvers, they give the surface of Frank Lloyd Wright's design a spinelike texture, much like the thistles and prairie flowers that inspired the architect throughout his life. (Left, courtesy of Price Tower Arts Center, 2003.16.115; below, courtesy of Price Tower Arts Center, 2003.16.119.)

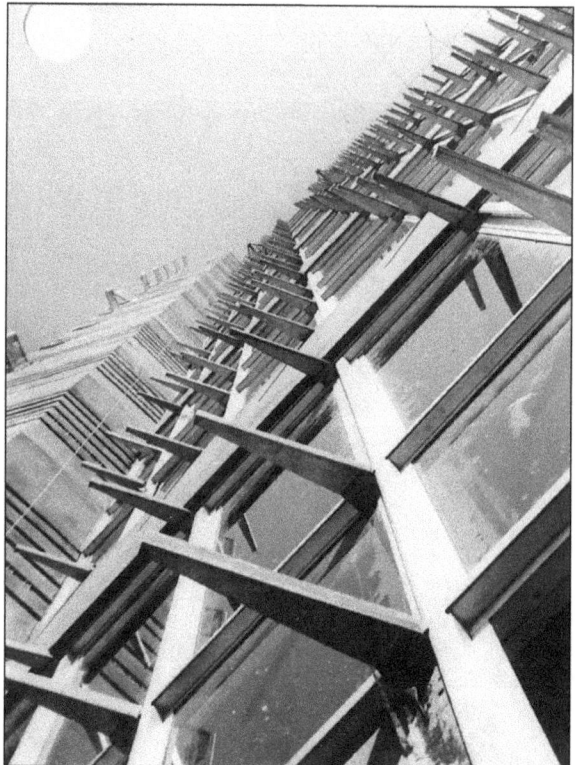

The aluminum-framed louver windows of the Price Tower office quadrants provided an expanse of light as well as ventilation to the office interiors. The cantilevered method of construction allowed for corner windows—glass meeting glass—that had become a favored feature of Wright to promote his "breaking of the box." (Courtesy of Price Tower Arts Center, 2003.16.111.)

The spiraling five-sided skylight replaced the original concept of a rooftop fountain for the two-story tenant wing and was also framed in aluminum. Photographed prior to the installation of its translucent glass panels, the taller structure, with its triangular exterior staircase, is visible overhead. (Courtesy of Price Tower Arts Center, 2003.16.123.)

A view from the southwest shows the dynamic elevations created by Frank Lloyd Wright's arrangement of horizontal and vertical architectural elements. Its horizontality is reinforced, illustrating the tie to the landscape, while simultaneously celebrating its verticality and marking the mid-century building as a truly "modern" skyscraper. (Courtesy of Price Tower Arts Center, 2003.16.083.)

A spire of patinated embossed copper over a steel core was designed for the top of the Price Tower, and the small roof surface and length of the spire made it necessary to complete the decorative element on the ground. The piece was assembled and its copper patinated before it was hoisted to the upper floors for final placement. (Courtesy of Price Tower Arts Center, 2003.16.167.)

The 30-foot-long, patinated copper spire was raised to its final position at the top of the Price Tower in August 1955, bringing the overall height to 221 feet. The spire was designed by Wright as a decorative element, lit by incandescent bulbs that were set into the diamond-shaped openings, but it was later used for radio and television reception. With the building's aluminum window frames now set into place—horizontal windows for the office quadrants, vertical windows for the double-height apartments—the application of the patinated louvers on the exterior could begin. (Above, courtesy of Price Tower Arts Center, 2003.16.075; below, courtesy of Price Tower Arts Center, 2003.16.112.)

Raised into place by a crane, the patinated copper spire was attached to the Price Tower with steel dowels and set away from the building just enough to create a ladder for maintenance workers to attend to the light bulbs set within it. (Courtesy of Price Tower Arts Center, 2003.16.131.)

Landscaped terraces were designed by Frank Lloyd Wright to provide even those working on upper floors with a sense of being tied to the prairie land surrounding Bartlesville. Potted trees, such as this for the rooftop dining terraces, also drew the curiosity of more than one street-level passerby. (Courtesy of Price Tower Arts Center, 2003.16.165.)

The ever-changing mood of the Price Tower, as well as its impact upon the skyline of Bartlesville, is made apparent in this pair of photographs taken in late 1955. At right, looking toward the spine of the elevation's exterior staircase, the horizontal bands of the office quadrant windows make the Price Tower appear squat and heavy. However, viewed from the west, below, the apartment quadrant's vertical windows elongate and slenderize it. This unpredictable aspect of Wright's design for the Price Tower, in combination with its materials and ornamental detailing, were uncharacteristic of "modern" skyscrapers of the 1950s, ensuring that no matter from what direction the tower was approached it was always visually compelling. (Right, courtesy of Price Tower Arts Center, 2003.16.194; below, courtesy of Price Tower Arts Center, 2003.16.196.)

A narrow lighted drive-through passageway linked the commercial and residential parking areas of the Price Tower and, in addition to the numerous glass windows, also provided another point of transparency through the building. This view, taken from the south elevation, shows the tunnel and the entrance to the caretaker's apartment, which was located beneath the perforated walls of the air-conditioning room at right. (Courtesy of Price Tower Arts Center, 2003.16.198.)

The commercial entrance to the Price Tower included a covered parking area, shown left with plantings covering its top, and a low canopy clad in patinated, embossed copper panels. The dramatic cantilevered effect of the tower's upper floors can be seen at right, their weight seemingly balanced upon a block of aluminum-framed windows. (Courtesy of Price Tower Arts Center, 2003.16.199.)

The modernity of Frank Lloyd Wright's Price Tower was fully realized at night, when each office and apartment in the building was lit and it "came to life" as a multiuse urban high rise. While the impact of an electrified "tree" would certainly have been lost in a larger urban "forest," like Chicago or New York City, where the tower had its origins, the Price Company's progressive promise of post–World War II architecture in Bartlesville was dramatically displayed and visible from nearly 15 miles away. The twinkling lights of the Price Tower's illuminated spire and the raking shadows of the spot-lit upper floors, along with the ground-level exterior lighting, provided a beacon of sorts that drew one to the city's center, a feature certainly appreciated by its architect as well as his client. (Courtesy of Price Tower Arts Center, 2003.16.220.)

Although the H. C. Price Company had occupied their new building since late 1955, the official public opening was held February 8–10, 1956. A seemingly endless line of visitors wrapped around the building and north along Dewey Avenue as 12,578 people came to view the "tree that escaped the crowded forest" those first three days. Tours were lead by Price Company employees and community volunteers who regaled their guests with facts about the tower's construction, its architect, and its patron. Many of the office spaces were also open for tours, as were the two-story furnished apartments whose efficient organization, built-in furnishings, and compact room arrangements were baffling to some. (Above, courtesy of Price Tower Arts Center, 2003.16.232; below, courtesy of Price Tower Arts Center, 2003.16.242.)

Harold Price Sr. and his son Harold Jr. welcomed Frank Lloyd Wright to the ribbon-cutting ceremony, officially opening the Price Tower to the public, where each man addressed the crowds from the terrace over the main entrance. Wright spoke of a "fresh realization of the modern advantages of architecture" and "release of the skyscraper from slavery," alluding to the importance of his building within the modern architecture movement. Reporters from across the country captured visitor reactions to the angular geometry of the interiors, the four small self-service Otis elevators, and the views of the Oklahoma prairie from the upper floors. (Above, courtesy of Price Tower Arts Center, 2003.16.234; below, courtesy of Price Tower Arts Center, 2003.16.238.)

The commercial lobby, inside the Price Tower's main entrance, was where visitors were introduced to Frank Lloyd Wright's geometric module—an equilateral triangle—that served as inspiration for the building's light fixtures, ventilation grilles, and interior columns. The mezzanine gallery connected the second floor of the 19-story tower to its two-story wing and provided a strong horizontal element to an otherwise vertical interior. (Courtesy of Price Tower Arts Center, 2003.16.257.)

The elevator lobby on each of the Price Tower's 19 floors marked the center point of the building's floor plan. An inlaid bronze medallion bearing the company logo—HCPCo—was mimicked by a lighted ceiling fixture and one's ability to see through the adjacent offices was part of Wright's intention of bringing the prairie landscape, albeit visually, to the interior of his skyscraper. (Courtesy of Price Tower Arts Center, 2003.16.285.)

When the H. C. Price Company took possession of the building in late 1955, the company's corporate apartment on the 17th and 18th floors had a decidedly minimalist Japanese-inspired decor. In the living area, a large painted screen was placed over the built-in Philippine mahogany desk and silk draperies, in a pattern from Frank Lloyd Wright's Taliesin line of wallpapers and fabrics for the F. Schumacher Company, New York City, hung from the double-height peach-tinted windows. Moveable furniture, such as the Philippine mahogany coffee table and upholstered hassock seating, was arranged in a casual fashion upon the incised Cherokee red pigmented concrete floors. At the desk was a cast-aluminum stenographer's chair, designed by Wright and manufactured by Blue Stem Foundry in nearby Dewey. The patinated, embossed copper frieze along the face of the mezzanine's parapet was the same as what was used on the building's exterior, reinforcing one of Wright's architectural tenets—that the exterior and interior, even in a tall building, should relate to each other. (Courtesy of Price Tower Arts Center, 2003.16.289.)

By February 1956, however, the interior of the Price Company corporate apartment was substantially updated to include an off-white wool area rug, painted geometric wall mural, moveable (and presumably more comfortable) lounge chairs from Frank Lloyd Wright's line of furniture for Heritage-Henredon, pink and coral abstract-patterned draperies, and brick-red colored upholstery fabrics—both from his Taliesin line of wallpapers and fabrics for the F. Schumacher Company of New York City. The cast aluminum stenographer's chair has been replaced with a dining chair, its full-length spine a reflection of the tower's triangular exterior staircase. The abstract wall mural, named *The Blue Moon* by Wright, was signed and dated by the architect and engaged the Philippine mahogany wall shelving to the right of the gas-burning fireplace. Its blue painted demilune mirror was also thought to symbolize the relationship between Price and Wright—that "once in a blue moon there exists the perfect client, the perfect architect, and the perfect building." (Courtesy of Price Tower Arts Center, 2003.16.295.)

The dining area of the Price Company corporate apartment changed as well, mostly to reflect the shift in design schemes as it was on the same level of the apartment as the living area. In the 1955 interior, the silk draperies can be seen, although curiously they do not cover the single window beneath the bedroom mezzanine. Two shelves above the angular dining table are sparsely filed with dinnerware and accessories and the use of cast aluminum stenographer's chairs at the dining table may indicate either that this was the intended chair design for the apartment interiors or, more likely, that the dining chairs had not yet been produced. The doors to the kitchen (with push plate) and powder room (with door knob) are constructed using the same Philippine mahogany as the built-in and moveable furniture. The diamond pattern of the upholstery fabric is shown on the banquette sofa cushions, and was selected, as were the draperies, from Wright's Taliesin line of fabrics and wallpapers for the F. Schumacher Company, New York City. (Courtesy of Price Tower Arts Center, 2003.16.289.)

When the Price Tower opened for its public viewing in February 1956, several changes to the dining area of the Price Company corporate apartment were in place. Included in the upgrades to the interior were two additional wall shelves above the built-in dining table and a mirror between the lowest shelf and the table's surface, visually projecting it through the wall plane. The wool area rug was cut to fit around the dining table's intricate angles and a television placed under the window, with several inches of built-in Philippine mahogany wall shelving removed to accommodate its size. The drapery fabric, selected from Frank Lloyd Wright's 1955 Taliesin line of textiles for the F. Schumacher Company, New York City, replaced the silk and was used on cushion tops for the hassocks. The cast aluminum chair styles changed as well, with the Wright-designed dining chair version with elongated spine replacing the stenographer's chairs. The wall above the dining table was painted a turquoise color to balance the multicolored wall mural across the room. (Courtesy of Price Tower Arts Center, 2003.16.294.)

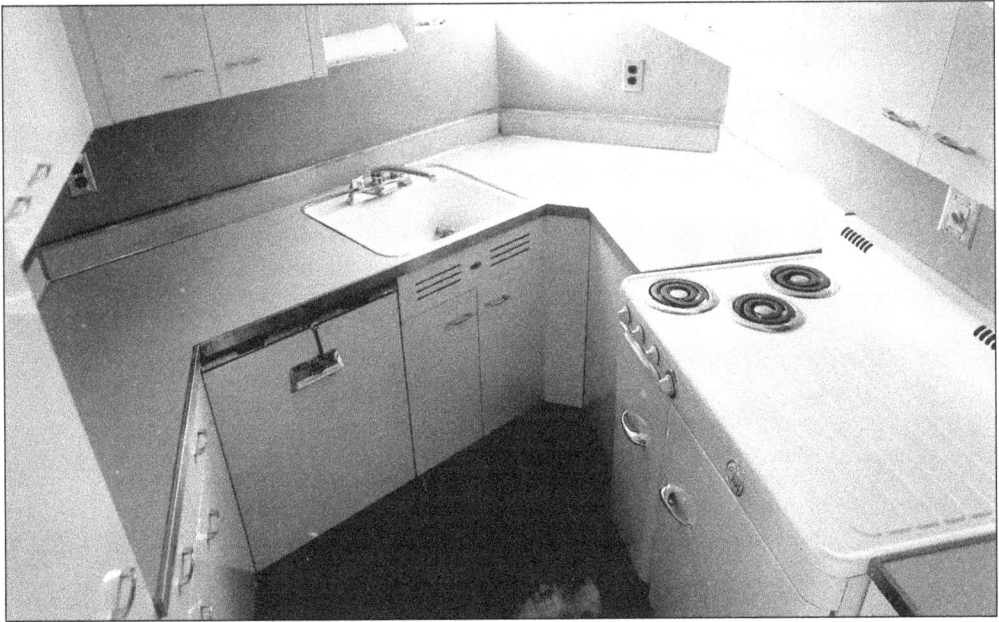

Each apartment in the Price Tower was designed with a small efficiency-style kitchen. Easy to use by one person, who realistically had everything within arm's reach, the kitchen also featured up-to-the-minute conveniences such as a top-loading dishwasher, refrigerator-oven unit, and rubbish chute to the basement. The painted metal cabinets and laminate countertops were durable and made cleaning easy. (Courtesy of Price Tower Arts Center, 2003.16.290.)

The bedroom mezzanine of each apartment was designed for a large bedroom and a smaller child's room with built-in bed and storage. The Price Company corporate apartment's bedroom had many of the same built-in furnishings as the living level below, including storage and wall shelving edged in half-round aluminum trim. (Courtesy of Price Tower Arts Center, 2003.16.286.)

Harold Price Sr.'s penthouse executive office suite was a double-height space featuring large expanses of window glass and a wood-burning fireplace. The decor of the 19th-floor interior was atypical of most 1950s office buildings and it included a large glass and mirror wall mural on the room's east wall that reinforced the triangular geometry of Frank Lloyd Wright's Price Tower plan. (Courtesy of Price Tower Arts Center, 2003.16.260.)

Price's office wall mural was designed by Eugene Masselink, under the direction of Wright. Masselink, one of Wright's senior apprentices, also installed the mural and is shown (in light colored shirt) working with an unknown assistant to lay down the guidelines for the mural's painted glass, colored glass, and gold leaf elements upon the field of silver mirror glass. (Courtesy of Price Tower Arts Center, 2003.16.268.)

Wright designed four versions of a basic chair style made of sand-cast aluminum, each upholstered in one of the architect's 1955 Taliesin line of textiles for the F. Schumacher Company of New York City. Although Wright attempted to have the chairs manufactured by more than one large office-furniture company, it was Blue Stem Foundry in nearby Dewey that was able to meet his exacting standards. The frame of each chair was a skeleton of silver painted aluminum and featured a hexagonal back cushion and a hexagonal seat pan that rested into the frame like a jewel into a ring setting. The casual chair, shown here with and without its upholstery, was joined by an executive's chair, a stenographer's chair (see page 75), and a dining chair (see page 74). (Right, courtesy of Price Tower Arts Center, 2003.16.281; below, courtesy of Price Tower Arts Center, 2003.16.282.)

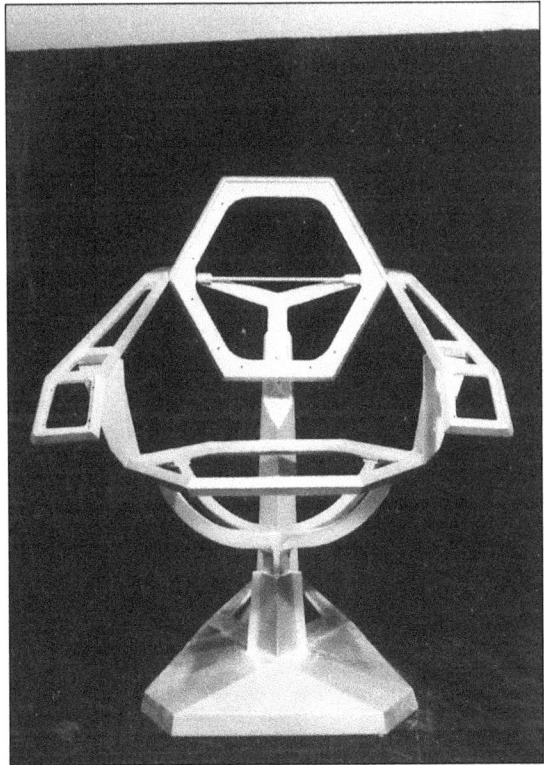

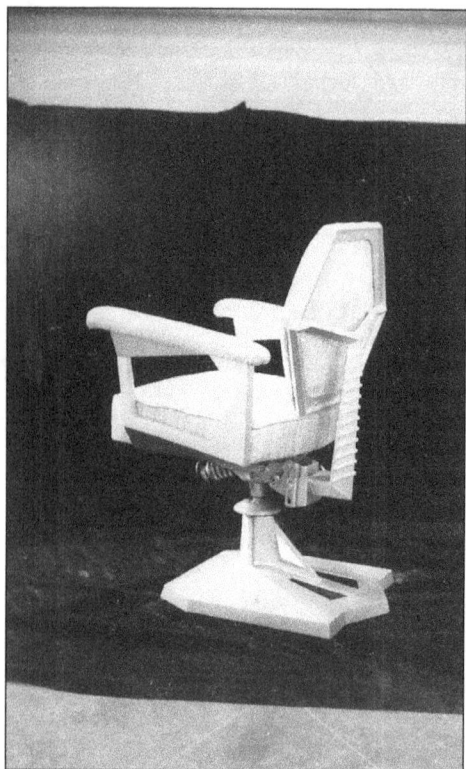

The executive's and stenographer's version of the Price Tower chairs featured a shortened spine, allowing the seats to swivel while the base remained firmly positioned. The executive's chair (shown at left) was only "half Wright" as the seat pan was removed from a store-bought reclining office chair. This was then retrofitted to the base and back manufactured by Blue Stem Foundry and gave the Price Company's executives the ability to recline to a lounging position. The stenographer's chair (below) retained the hexagonal seat of the casual and dining chair styles, although provided little in the way of comfort for the user group who spent the most time in them. The back tilted to allow for some flexibility, but these chairs were often discarded once more ergonomic designs became available. (Left, courtesy of Price Tower Arts Center, 2003.16.279; below, courtesy of Price Tower Arts Center, 2003.16.276.)

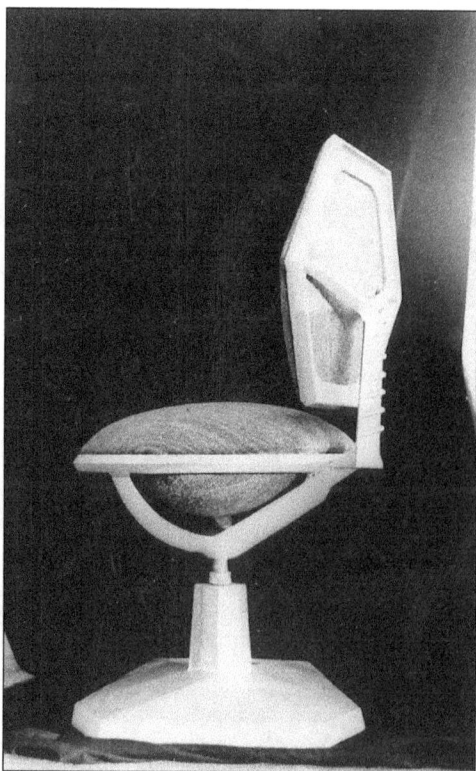

The office interiors were designed for flexibility and to be used by a variety of tenants. Interior wood and glass partition walls allowed for easy reconfiguration and privacy as needed. The angles of the partition walls and the built-in desks were still designed to fall upon Wright's incised angular floor grid and finishes such as window treatments and carpeting were frowned upon. (Courtesy of Price Tower Arts Center, 2003.16.292.)

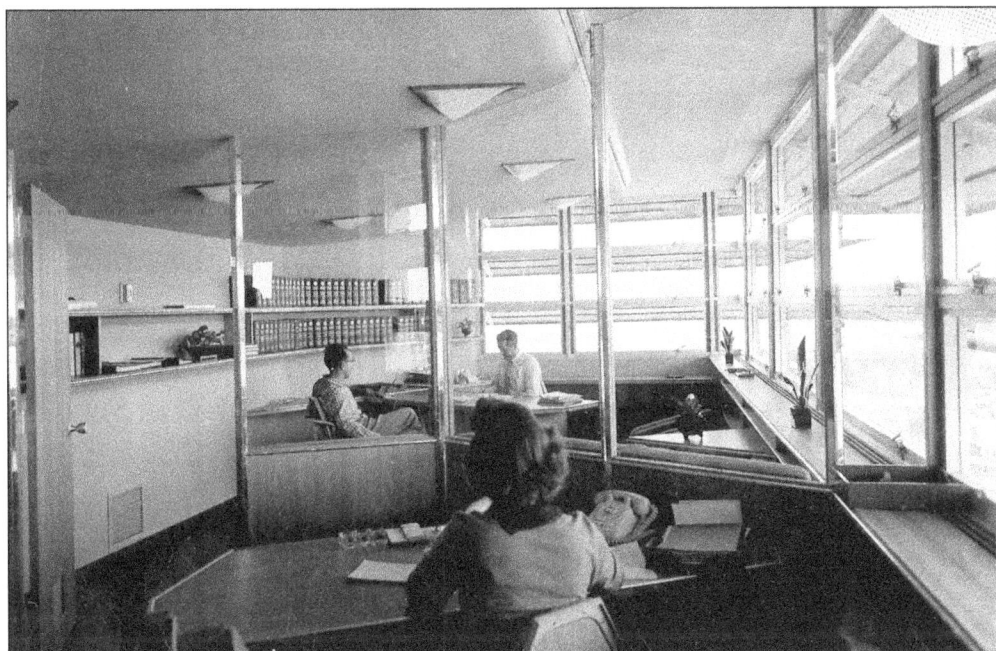

A typical H. C. Price Company interior utilized a range of built-in and temporary furnishings. The partition walls were used to create smaller private offices within a quadrant, while also maintaining the transparency feature of Wright's skyscraper, ensuring all occupants had an office with a view. (Courtesy of Price Tower Arts Center, 2003.16.293.)

PUBLIC SERVICE *NEWS*

FEBRUARY ★ 1956

BARTLESVILLE AREA MANAGER W. D. McGINLEY (below) opens the door for a customer to enter the beautiful and modern Public Service Bartlesville offices in the new Price Tower building (right). This 19-story skyscraper of a revolutionary new architecture was designed by the famous Frank Lloyd Wright. For the story of Public Service in the Price Tower see pages 2 to 6.

While a furniture and finishes package was designed by Frank Lloyd Wright for the tenants of the Price Tower, not all chose to utilize (or purchase) his site-specific designs. The second-largest tenant in the tower was the Public Service Company of Oklahoma, the area's public utilities offices, which occupied the two-story wing. While they were proud to be associated with the Price Tower, as shown in these images from their February 1956 newsletter, the relatively stark interiors were furnished with pre-made teller units and freestanding desks—all of which may have been used in the Public Service Company's previous facility. The drapery panels shown were not chosen from Wright's 1955 Taliesin line for Schumacher, offering some insight in the role in which Wright and the Price Company played with regard to maintaining a continuous decoration scheme throughout the building. (Courtesy of the ConocoPhillips Corporate Archives.)

Downtown Bartlesville gained its most important public arts venue with the addition of a community center that would host a wide variety of small- and large-scale performances and events. The Bartlesville Community Center, designed by Taliesin Associated Architects of Scottsdale, Arizona, the firm headed by Frank Lloyd Wright's former apprentice and son-in-law, William Wesley Peters, was constructed in a site diagonally across the street from the Price Tower and opened to the public in 1982. When the firm was commissioned four years earlier, it was given neither budget nor details of what should be included in the center's facility. The result, following analyses of surveys mailed to potential users, was a multipurpose design flexible enough to be built in stages at the cost of $13.5 million and included public artwork, shaded benches, and water features. (Courtesy of the Bartlesville Community Center.)

The graceful curves of the community center's facade, its sheltered balcony promenade, and the cantilevered roof structure required a deep foundation, similarly curved and constructed of reinforced concrete. The deep foundation allowed for lower-level necessities such as boiler room and storage, but also for small meeting and banquet rooms, reached via a gently sloping interior ramp. The top photograph shows curved plywood forms in place as they await the pouring of liquid concrete with lengths of reinforcing bars laying nearby. Below, with plywood forms removed, the walls take on a patchwork appearance and once completed, reach street level and the raising of the upper structure. (Courtesy of the Bartlesville Community Center.)

Structural engineering for the Bartlesville Community Center was contracted to the Chicago firm of Wilson, Andros, Roberts, and Noll, which received a Best Structure Award by the Illinois Structural Engineering Association in 1981. Responsible for the building's substructure and structural framing, the award was also based upon the combined use of steel, reinforced concrete, and brick. The monolithic east elevation of the center, above, conceals the backstage area seen in the lower image framed by steel girders. The sloping floor of the auditorium is at center with the far wall and exterior balconies yet to be added. (Courtesy of the Bartlesville Community Center.)

Taken from the upper floors of the Price Tower, a pair of photographs illustrates the arcing west elevation of the Bartlesville Community Center as scaffolding (above) and the reinforced concrete's plywood forms are erected in the summer of 1980. By the following year, shown below, the clamshell-like roof was in place and landscaping had begun on the plaza and parking areas to the west of the center. When completed, the tree-lined sidewalk and built-in concrete benches provided visitors with a comfortable place to relax after a performance or on a sunny afternoon. The community center's circular fountain and planter, inherent in many of Taliesin's designs, offered visual interest and was later adorned with *Suspended Moment*, an 11-foot bronze sculpture designed by Taliesin fellow Heloise Swabeck and donated to the community center by Harold Price Jr. (Courtesy of the Bartlesville Community Center.)

The north elevation of the Bartlesville Community Center (above) featured the entrance to a below-grade box office lobby entrance and a stage-level service court accessible by a gentle ramp. The steeply sloping roof, a modified pagoda design, was trimmed with spherical lighting fixtures, which when lit create a dramatic "strand of pearls" across the arcing west facade. The west elevation (below) included a second lobby entrance as well as a series of recessed doors opening into the 6,000-square-foot community center hall that provided unencumbered access to the parking lot. The inverted arches of the balcony level gave those utilizing the space uniquely framed views of the downtown skyline. (Courtesy of the Bartlesville Community Center.)

The east elevation (above) of the Bartlesville Community Center was designed as a monolithic counterpoint to the arcing elevations on the west side. Housed in the rectilinear volumes were the stage workshop, dressing rooms, and emergency exit staircase and the height designed to accommodate the theatrical lighting and raised stage curtains. The south elevation (below) served as the street side entrance, where a third lobby directed visitors into the auditorium or to the administration offices. The decorative elements provided by Taliesin Associated Architects included expanded signage, its projected profile casting shadows onto the redbrick exterior and a series of semicircular grilles that offer viewers a hint at the geometric theme of the overall design. (Courtesy of the Bartlesville Community Center.)

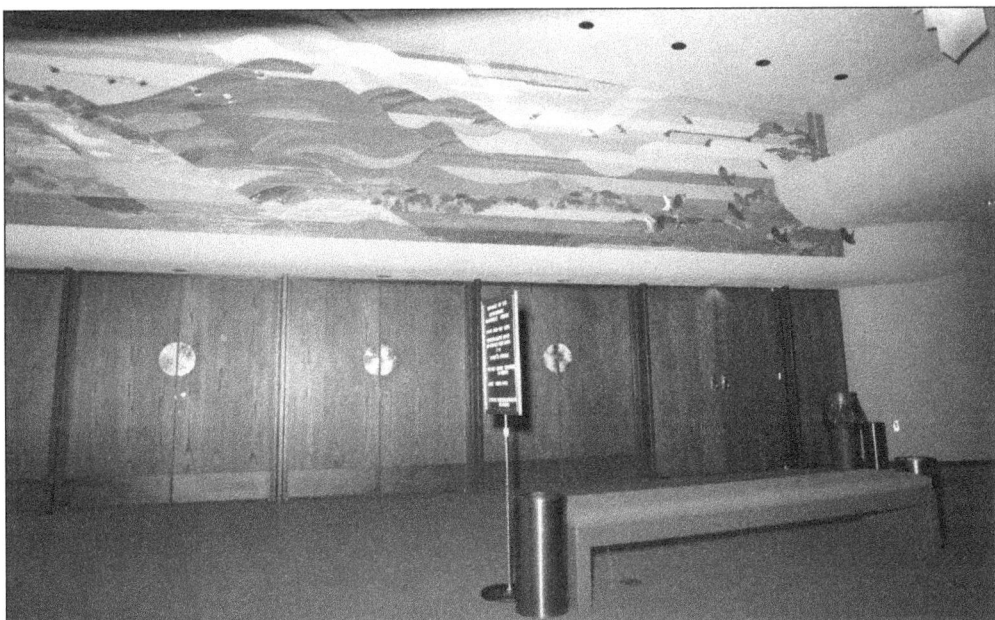

The west lobby featured a 25-foot-long cloisonné mural designed by Taliesin fellow Heloise Swaback and installed in 1981 by Mitzi Dzivi Doliber. Meant to depict the northeastern Oklahoma landscape over four seasons, the mural—of colored enamel tiles and copper and brass framing—was the largest example of the cloisonné technique in the world. (Courtesy of the Bartlesville Community Center.)

Entering via portal doors off of a pair of stairways on each side of the auditorium, a visitor's procession upward was enhanced by a fluted ceiling treatment that captured sound as well as prevented vertigo while ascending the low-rising stairs. The doorway to each row was set within a pair of arcing walls, the handrails following the curve and gently directing visitors inward. (Courtesy of the Bartlesville Community Center.)

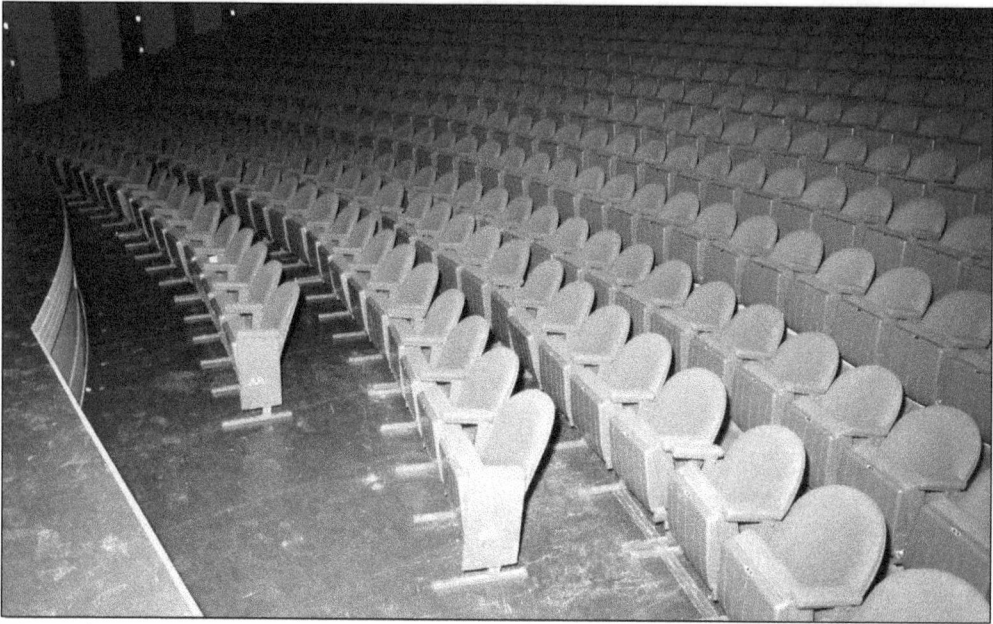

The auditorium interior included seating for up to 1,800 persons spread across 28 rows of continental-style seating and, if needed, three rows of additional seating on the orchestra lift. Taliesin's design for the interior was such that there was never a bad seat in the house—the building's engineering eliminated the necessity of interior columns and the seat-back-to-seat-back depth a generous 42 inches. (Courtesy of the Bartlesville Community Center.)

Iciclelike crystalline chandeliers in the community center hall added visual interest to the flexible interior, meant to serve groups of 20 to 500 for meetings, banquets, receptions, and trade shows. An adjacent series of meeting rooms allowed for break-away meeting spaces and a large catering kitchen was accessible to the exterior service court for deliveries. (Courtesy of the Bartlesville Community Center.)

Three

MODERN INDUSTRY
THE PHILLIPS PETROLEUM COMPANY
BUILDS DOWNTOWN

It is difficult to imagine what life was like when Frank Phillips moved to Bartlesville from Creston, Iowa, in 1903. The city was in the early boom years, and during these years a century ago, it enjoyed unusual success. The population at the end of the 19th century was 698, and by 1950, it would be nearly 20,000—a testament to the oil industry that brought many here, and the quality of life that gave them reason to stay.

While the city was named for its founder Jacob Bartles, a merchant who purchased a gristmill on the shore of the Caney River in 1875, it was not long before Bartlesville became synonymous with oil in general and the Phillips Petroleum Company in particular. Other large oil corporations came and left, but the Phillips Petroleum Company gave Bartlesville its nickname, "the town that oil built," in great part by building it itself. This chapter explores the impact of one company on the architectural heritage of Bartlesville over nearly six decades, and shows its consistent attention to the needs of not only the company and its employees, but of the economic and cultural impact on the community overall.

Beginning with the Adams Building in 1950 through to the Phillips Plaza Building in 1987, Phillips Petroleum Company architecture after World War II was more than merely accommodating employees into efficient work environments. The care that the company has shown for its employees is exhibited in the buildings themselves. The gymnasium and sports facilities incorporated into the plans for the Adams Building are the most obvious, but the opening of the Phillips Apartment Hotel satisfied a need more essential, that of accessible and affordable housing for employees.

Designed along with the Phillips Plaza Building were public gardens and pathways surrounding it—a clear indication that the company felt a building's beauty extended beyond the physical walls. The landscaped areas continue to provide access to seasonal flowers, fountains, and enjoyable lunch spots. In their way, they also serve as reminders of the Oklahoma prairie from which the oil industry, and Phillips Petroleum Company, began.

Phillips Petroleum Company was incorporated by brothers Frank and Lee Eldas Phillips in 1917, consolidated from their numerous individual oil holdings and in the light of the oil boom years of World War I. The company grew exponentially—from 27 employees in 1917 to nearly 25,000 at the end of 1958—and in 1927, the firm moved from its second floor offices on Third Street (now Frank Phillips Boulevard) to a new seven-story building designed by the firm of Keene and Simpson, Kansas City, on the block bordered by Johnstone and Keeler Avenues and Third and Fourth Streets. In 1930, the architects added an eighth floor and tower, and the building became known as the Frank Phillips Building, the tower of which is the only remaining feature. In 1939, at age 65, Frank Phillips retired as president of Phillips Petroleum Company, and Kenneth "Boots" Adams was chosen to succeed him, making Frank Phillips the first chairman of the board, a position he held until the year before his death in 1950. (Courtesy of the Bartlesville Area History Museum.)

In 1949, construction was underway on a new 12-story multipurpose building. Designed by the Kansas City, Missouri, architectural firm of Neville and Sharp, the building was named in honor of the Phillips Petroleum Company chief executive officer and continues to be known as the Adams Building. Encompassing an entire city block, the building opened for occupancy in 1950, the same year as Frank Phillips's death, and combined employees from 38 different offices into one centralized complex. The rectilinear high-rise office building, a typical example of 1950s modernism, was constructed of poured concrete piers and slabs, and faced in reddish brick, its Keeler Street entrance is marked by a double-height portico. (Courtesy of the ConocoPhillips Corporate Archives.)

The Keeler Avenue elevation of the Adams Building best expresses the modernity of the 12-story building, providing the Phillips Petroleum Company with a symbol of strength and financial success in the years following World War II. The Adams Building, designed and constructed at a cost of $8.735 million, was the tallest building in Bartlesville and with 457,000 square feet of utilizable space, its largest in area. The 12-story high-rise took up only half of the city block, however, and a lower two-story wing to the rear housed the company's athletic facilities and mechanical services. (Above, courtesy of the Bartlesville Area History Museum; left, courtesy of the ConocoPhillips Corporate Archives.)

The rear of the Adams Building was decidedly used for more utilitarian functions but nonetheless was designed in a consistent manner as the taller structure through its series of marching second-story square windows, recessed and framed in the same technique and materials as the street-level entrances and larger double-height windows. The Jennings Avenue elevation, shown below, included the entrance to the Phillips Gymnasium, its facade punctuated by three circular windows and broad entry. The Phillips Gymnasium was designed to include a field house, swimming pool, and gymnasium facilities, as well as social rooms for the Frank Phillips Men's Club and the Jane Phillips Society. (Courtesy of the ConocoPhillips Corporate Archives.)

The Adams Building provided Phillips Petroleum Company employees with a variety of facilities, including assembly rooms, conference rooms, a library, a medical center, barber shop, and separate club rooms for the company's Frank Phillips Men's Club and the Jane Phillips Sorority. The cafeteria (above) fed between 800 and 1,200 employees and was furnished with small tables that could be joined to form various seating configurations. The sports facilities included a gymnasium, was designed to seat 3,000 sports fans, and was home to the company's famed Bartlesville Phillips 66ers basketball team. The team, which recorded 1,543 wins and 271 losses, also yielded four company presidents and three vice presidents. (Courtesy of the ConocoPhillips Corporate Archives.)

In 1948, while the Adams Building was being constructed, plans were developed for an apartment building, intended to relieve the housing shortage that plagued Bartlesville following World War II. Designed by the Kansas City, Missouri, architectural firm of Gentry and Voskamp, the Phillips Apartment Hotel was built on the west side of Johnstone Avenue between Eighth and Ninth Streets, and was within walking distance to the Phillips Petroleum Company campus, yet part of the tree-lined residential neighborhood south of Seventh Street (now Adams Street). As groundbreaking plans began, safety barriers were erected in November 1948 in anticipation of excavation a month later. (Courtesy of Price Tower Arts Center Archives.)

Construction of the seven-story Phillips Apartment Hotel was half complete in 1949 (above), slowing rising above treetops, and when completed, was among the tallest buildings in downtown Bartlesville. Manhattan Construction Company of Muskogee served as general contractor for the project, in addition to the Adams Building. The apartment building (shown below in early 1950) was fully air-conditioned, and its amenities included a roof-top sun deck, self-service laundry, and modern self-service elevators. The building was clad in light-colored brick and windows were framed in aluminum. (Above, courtesy of Price Tower Arts Center Archives; below, courtesy of the Bartlesville Area History Museum.)

When the Phillips Apartment Hotel opened for tenants in June 1950, it provided 206 furnished residential units in a variety of configurations. Twenty-eight five-room efficiency apartments, 84 four-room efficiency apartments, and 66 four-room efficiencies were supplemented by 28 hotel rooms. The units were supplied with forced-air heating and garbage was collected daily. The efficiency apartments featured private baths and streamlined kitchens with porcelain cabinets, ranges, and refrigerators. The rent for the apartments began at $75 a month and hotel rooms cost $6 per night. (Above, courtesy of Price Tower Arts Center Archives; below, courtesy of the ConocoPhillips Corporate Archives.)

Residents and guests of the Phillips Apartment Hotel were welcomed by a brightly lit modern lobby (above), appointed with marble floors and walls and aluminum railing and window and door frames. A typical hotel room (below) was spacious with large bed, easy chair, desk, and large windows overlooking downtown Bartlesville. The interior of the apartment hotel was decorated in 14 schemes that included draperies, wall-to-wall carpet, lamps, upholstered furnishings, and framed photographs. The varied quantity of decorating schemes also meant that no two apartments of the same color scheme were adjacent to one another. The Phillips Apartment Hotel began operating as Hotel Phillips in 1980 and its apartments were converted to 156 luxury guest rooms and suites. (Courtesy of the Bartlesville Area History Museum.)

The addition of the Phillips Petroleum Company's Phillips Building in downtown Bartlesville added another example of modernistic architecture to the skyline. At 19 stories, it became the tallest building in the city, and provided a dramatic counterpoint to another building that shared a similar size footprint—the First National Bank of Bartlesville, constructed at the same time directly to the tower's north. Los Angeles architectural firm Welton Becket Associates designed the Phillips Building, as well as the First National Bank in 1962, and both opened in mid-1964. (Above, courtesy of the ConocoPhillips Corporate Archives; below, courtesy of the Bartlesville Area History Museum.)

The "soberly handsome" Phillips Building, at 292 feet tall, was designed to contrast with the steel-and-glass skyscrapers typical of the 1950s and 1960s. Eighteen floors were cantilevered upon a glass-walled central core, creating an illusionary distribution of weight and dramatic recessed entrances to the building. The building served to house the executive offices for Phillips Petroleum Company, which occupied two full floors, and the materials overall reflected an appropriate upscale aesthetic. The lobby was finished with black terrazzo floors and teak walls with tangerine colored tufted sofas. Interior design was supervised by Mildred English, a Los Angeles interior design firm working in conjunction with Welton Becket Associates. (Courtesy of the Bartlesville Area History Museum.)

Researching new opportunities has always been part of the Phillips Petroleum Company's mission. Since the 1920s, the company explored new technologies in natural gas processing, oil refining, and specialized products and services that supplemented their already successful brands. Its growing interest in aviation, including designing aviation refueling trucks and the development of more efficient airplane fuels, which aided the company's plane *Woolaroc*, named after Frank Phillips's Osage Hills ranch, to make the first nonstop flight from the United States to Hawaii. The new Phillips Building provided exhibition space for many of the company's 40 years worth of achievements and gave visitors an opportunity to explore the company's numerous patented products including polyethylene plastics and high-density resins. These technologies were sold to manufacturers to use in packaging and containers, many of which were used to contain Phillips Petroleum's liquid goods. (Courtesy of the ConocoPhillips Corporate Archives.)

The architectonic exhibits also featured photographic displays of many of the Phillips Petroleum Company drilling and refinery sites, service stations, and research centers around the world. In 1964, when the Phillips Building opened, these would have included those in Oklahoma, Texas, Louisiana, Utah, Alaska, and Venezuela as well as those offshore. Packaging of the company's many products and designed objects such as signage, advertisements, gas station displays, uniform patches, and souvenirs were placed in display cases throughout the exhibition area. These items now serve as the basis for the Phillips Petroleum Company Museum. (Courtesy of the ConocoPhillips Corporate Archives.)

In 1977, Phillips Petroleum Company commissioned the Dallas architectural firm of Dahl, Braden, Jones, and Chapman to design its information center building, housing its information technology systems. Known for their contributions to the Dallas architectural community, the firm's work also included 26 buildings for the University of Texas at Austin, 32 stores for Sears, Roebuck and Company, and 15 prisons for the Texas Department of Corrections. Their design for Phillips Petroleum was remarkably monolithic in form, hiding much of the building's structure, as well as its function, from passersby. The unadorned brick exterior took on a sculptural quality, as if a series of interlocking puzzle pieces. (Courtesy of the ConocoPhillips Corporate Archives.)

Phillips Petroleum began plans for its 428,000-square-foot Plaza Office Building in the early 1980s, and by groundbreaking in June 1984, it was destined to become the largest facility for the company in Bartlesville. Designed to be flexible and efficient with offices and work stations for 1,500 employees, as well as generous conference spaces and filing rooms, the 15-story brick and limestone tower featured large bronze-tinted bay windows that flooded the spacious floor plans with natural light and were trimmed in limestone and copper. Furnishings were modern and enhanced the communications between departments. The Plaza Office Building's role within the company was to provide centralized facilities for five major groups of employees: human resources, exploration and production, Phillips 66 Natural Gas Company, corporate tax, and the corporate procurement and materials control division of engineering and services. (Courtesy of the ConocoPhillips Corporate Archives.)

Viewed from the east, the Phillips Petroleum Company's Plaza Office Building projected a "strong and distinctive" profile against the Oklahoma sky. The Plaza Office Building's exterior materials were also meant to harmonize with other downtown buildings, and three interior color schemes were rotated throughout the building. Surrounding parks were envisaged as links between the various company buildings, including a European-style walking street paved with patterned stone. A future expansion project included the partial demolition of the original Frank Phillips Building, retaining its historic tower, for the Tower Center, a four-story complex for food services, medical center, and three conference rooms. Designed by the firm of Hellmuth, Obata, and Kassabaum, of St. Louis, the Plaza Office Building opened to its first occupants in December 1986 and to the public for an open house in February 1987, and the Tower Center opened in August 1988. (Courtesy of the Bartlesville Area History Museum.)

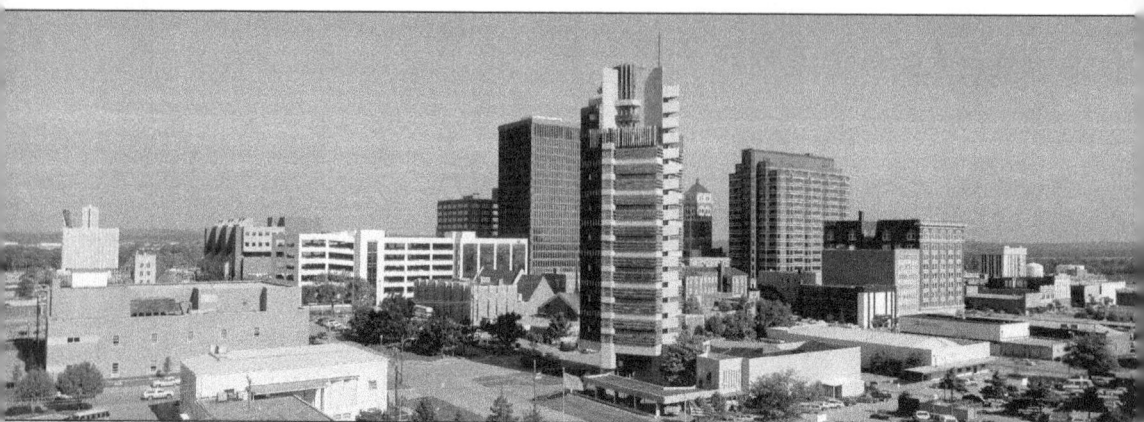

In 1981, the H. C. Price Company moved its corporate headquarters to Dallas, Texas, and the Phillips Petroleum Company purchased the Price Tower, adding yet another tall building to its campus. It was also an honored and award-winning structure as it was added to the National Register of Historic Places in 1974 and received the prestigious Twenty-Five Year Award from the American Institute of Architects in 1983, recognizing the enduring significance of Frank Lloyd Wright's design. In 1986, Phillips Petroleum Company invited the Landmark Preservation Council of Washington County to assume docent duties for tours of the Price Tower. The tower, however, was not fully utilized and after various initiatives to market it to prospective buyers, including plans for a condominium development, Phillips Petroleum Company refurbished Price Tower and in 2001 donated it to Price Tower Arts Center, a tenant since 1990. (Courtesy of the ConocoPhillips Corporate Archives.)

Four

BUILDINGS FOR EVERYDAY USE

BARTLESVILLE PUBLIC ARCHITECTURE

Attempting to categorize the vast amount of public buildings in Bartlesville can be a daunting task, and as many of them serve specialized purposes—schools, churches, libraries, banks—it can be easy to overlook their importance in a city's architectural heritage. This chapter will survey a selection of building types as a means of addressing the varied functional issues in architecture, especially those traits that make its function recognizable, and include a few that many have not before been seen or thought of as architecture.

To think of a city without a hospital, schools, or post office seems strange. Yet it is these types of buildings that define a city. As Bartlesville grew, so did the need for newer and larger facilities, those that educated, enlightened, cured, and entertained its citizens. Time spent in them may have been a matter of hours, days, a week, or a year making them feel less important than, say, a home, but public buildings are often given homey qualities through their color schemes or furnishings as a means of making them more appealing.

Expansion is often incorporated into the plans for new public buildings, and many of the following designs were conceived with the knowledge that as the city grew, there would need to be additions made. Nearly all of the public school buildings built in Bartlesville after World War II were expanded, as was the original 1939 College High (now Bartlesville High School), designed by John Duncan Forsyth in a streamlined moderne style. Subdivisions blossomed and with them the need for grocery stores, shopping centers, and gasoline stations, their presence so ubiquitous that they are often not considered. Churches, banks, and even the public library and post office experienced growing pains that necessitated new buildings to meet the demand of population growth.

The diversity of styles and influences is most apparent in the public buildings of Bartlesville. While much of the city built before 1945 was of an identifiable style using a small selection of materials, those after World War II looked to new industries and technologies, challenging the canon and expressing their modernity.

Bartlesville's second hospital, Jane Phillips Hospital, opened in 1952, four years after the death of Jane Gibson Phillips, wife of Phillips Petroleum Company founder Frank Phillips, in whose memory it was named. Prior to her death, Jane Phillips wished to see a maternity hospital established in Bartlesville, then home to the smaller Washington County Memorial Hospital, which opened in 1922 and included a nursing school. Advised of the need for more extensive facilities, the Frank Phillips Foundation engaged an architect to survey the best features and facilities of examples of hospitals throughout the Midwest, and the result was a design that permitted expansions based upon future population growth and patient needs. In 1958, once the 95-bed facility was operating successfully, its ownership was deeded to the Oklahoma Episcopal Diocese, who subsequently renamed it the Jane Phillips Episcopal Hospital. (Courtesy of the Bartlesville Area History Museum.)

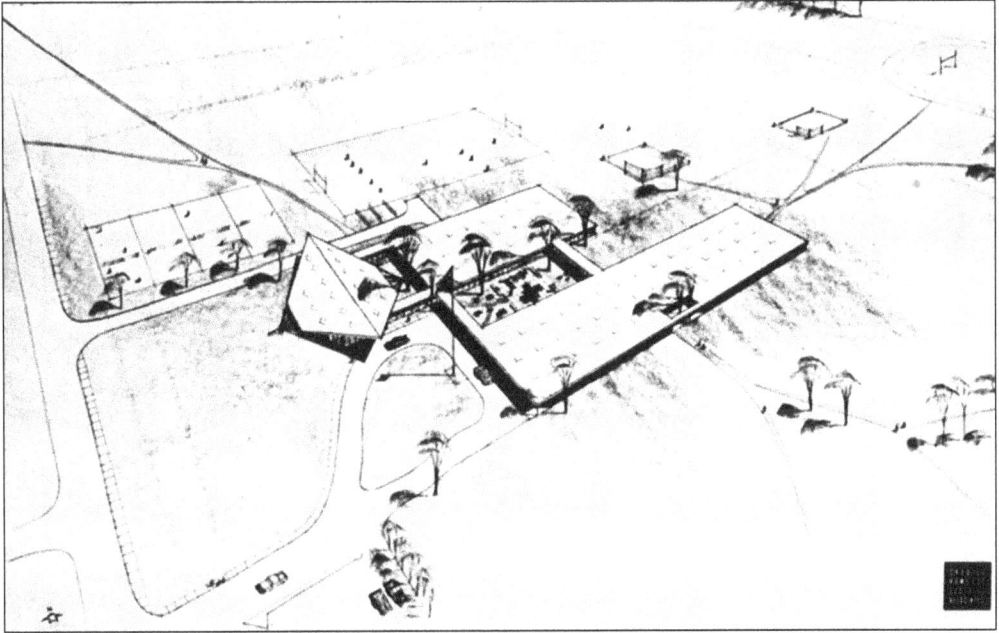

The Houston architectural firm Caudill Rowlett Scott and Associates was commissioned by the Bartlesville School District in 1958 to design Madison Junior High School (now Madison Middle School). Built upon a 50-acre site, it contained nine classrooms, administration areas, library, cafeteria, band room, choral room, gymnasium, industrial arts shops, science labs, art room, and home economics suite. The architectural program took the physical and emotional welfare of the students in mind, and utilized natural light, warm cheerful color schemes, multipurpose courtyards, informal snack bar, and acoustical ceiling materials. While the initial scheme was designed for 600 students, it was developed so that additions could be added to accommodate twice that number—first in 1960 and later in 1963, when the student population reached 1,000. (Courtesy of the Bartlesville Area History Museum.)

The United States Army Military District of Oklahoma dedicated the newly constructed Earnest L. Ripley Army Reserve Center, located on Washington Avenue, in June 1959. Ripley was raised in Bartlesville and graduated from Bartlesville High School before obtaining a degree in civil engineering at Oklahoma Agricultural and Mechanical College (now Oklahoma State University) in 1937. He was called to active duty in 1941 and killed in action four years later in Italy, with the rank of lieutenant colonel. The naming of the reserve center followed a year-long campaign to honor one of Bartlesville's deceased soldiers, and once opened, was home to 10 reserve units in the Washington County area. (Courtesy of the Bartlesville Area History Museum.)

Bruce Goff's 1959 design for the Redeemer Lutheran Church Education Building was initially part of a larger scheme that included a glass-cullet-encrusted sanctuary and ramped pathways crossing its surrounding moat. The less dramatic of the two buildings, the education center, was adapted and realized in reinforced concrete clad with flagstone and only dotted with glass cullets, except at its corners where they were piled upward in peaks. The random forms of its architectural materials were juxtaposed by square windows, turned on point, and a rectangular overhang supported by arrowlike brackets. (Above, courtesy of the Art Institute of Chicago; right, courtesy of Price Tower Arts Center Archives.)

After nearly 30 years at its location in the north wing of the Bartlesville Civic Center, the Bartlesville Public Library was expanded in 1960 to provide improved facilities to its nearly 14,000 annual users—a venture that saw great philanthropic and volunteer support. In 1960, armed with grant monies, the library opened a self-development center that included a fine arts room, reading lounge, and a current information room, and in 1961, the task of renovating the upstairs American Legion room into the community history room began. Housing local and regional historical resources and materials, the new history room paved the way for the formation of a 12-person historical commission, which named Margaret Teague Withers its inaugural curator in 1964. Twenty years later, this historical data for the Bartlesville area became the core of the current Bartlesville Area History Museum and Archives, which remained in the library until 2000. (Courtesy of the Bartlesville Area History Museum.)

The interior of the new Bartlesville Public Library addition was decidedly modern and included a spacious entryway, shown above, and an expansive reference room, shown below. The library's sleek materials—terrazzo flooring, plastic laminate surfaces, and metal shelving—were durable enough to withstand years of use and required low maintenance, while the furnishings were flexible enough to meet the needs of a variety of user groups. Interior glass partition walls allowed for visual transparency and natural light from the building's clerestory windows, supplemented with fluorescent cove lighting above the shelving. In the reference room, a monolithic lit ceiling provided the interior rooms with a reading-quality light level. (Courtesy of the Bartlesville Area History Museum.)

Cities Service Oil Company was established in Bartlesville in 1912, founded by banker and utilities multimillionaire Henry L. Doherty. Cities Service, a leader in petroleum research and oil and natural gas metering methods, slowly began buying smaller oil and gas operations and became the 10th largest oil company in the country by 1935. Like many of its competitors, Cities Service developed a corporate identity in its advertising, product graphics, and service station designs. The Cities Service station shown here on its opening day, around 1961, drew crowds to its location on Fourth Street and Osage Avenue, a few blocks from its corporate headquarters. Uniformed attendants pumped the company's premium 5-D gasoline, changed oil in specialized lubrication bays, and washed cars. In 1965, now named CITGO, the company moved its headquarters to Tulsa. (Courtesy of the Bartlesville Area History Museum.)

The spiraling staircase of Bruce Goff's 1963 Sooner Park Play Tower for Bartlesville's Sooner Park on the city's east side reached nearly five stories in height and once there, visitors were able to view the city from within a metallic mesh sphere. Progressing up the cylinder's spiral staircase was surely thrilling and the cantilevered steps gave one the feeling of walking on air. The design, commissioned by Mary Lou Price for the city, also featured a mobius strip and sand-castle elements at the base of the tower that are no longer extant. Adorning the tower were beaded cables connecting the sphere to the ground below. Currently closed to climbers, the play tower stands as one of Goff's few public works of sculpture and is reminiscent of the space-age era in which it was designed. (Courtesy of Price Tower Arts Center Archives.)

In April 1964, the First National Bank in Bartlesville moved into its new "striking, yet functional" 35,000-square-foot headquarters. Designed by Welton Becket Associates, famous for their modern business-like designs, the Los Angeles firm's body of work included a 13-story tower for Capital Records in 1956, the world's first circular office building, whose beacon spelled the word "Hollywood" in Morse code. Their design for Bartlesville was restrained, and drew upon classic architectural features. The window walls of the bank were 26-foot-tall panels of bronze-tinted glass, a color that was also seen in the embossed facade of the overhanging roof. Resting on a white marble plinth, it was adjacent to the newly opened Phillips Petroleum Company's Phillips Building, also designed by Welton Becket Associates. (Courtesy of the Bartlesville Area History Museum.)

The main lobby of the First National Bank was divided into two large areas, one for the commercial loan department (above) and a building-long teller line (below) that was topped with a 6,000-square-foot mezzanine. The commercial loan department also featured glass enclosed offices for the bank's officers and chairman of the board, work stations for loan officers, and a customer lounge seating area. The teller line was supplemented by three drive-through banking lanes that offered closed-circuit two-way television communication between customer and teller. Escalators provided access to and from the bank's concourse level. (Courtesy of the Bartlesville Area History Museum.)

The First National Bank of Bartlesville was purchased by Frank Phillips in 1920, at a time when the oilman strongly considered a career in banking rather than oil. Over the years, his cordial business relationships with many of the era's notorious bank bandits and train robbers ensured his bank would never be a target, although protective measures were necessary. In 1964, one of the most complicated challenges presented to the architects, and a curiosity for onlookers, was the relocation of the original "burglarproof" Herring-Hall-Marvin Safe Company vault door to the new building's main lobby cash vault. Located in the southeast corner of the ground floor, the door was nearly seven feet in diameter and was a secure location for the bank's daily cash and documentation as much as a showpiece. In addition to the main floor's vault, a concourse-level safe deposit vault with 2,200 boxes was engineered for future expansion as the bank's clientele grew. (Courtesy of the Bartlesville Area History Museum.)

The clear span ceiling of the First National Bank of Bartlesville was dotted with over 1,000 individually recessed lights, creating a dramatic nighttime expression of modernity when lit. The light bounced off of the white ceiling as well as the white marble floor heightening the brilliant effect. The building's bronze-glass window wall became transparent when lit from within, an illusion that made the roof appear to float, and rows of the same recessed lights extended beyond the window wall to light the sidewalk and adjacent plaza. Later home to the Bartlesville headquarters of the WestStar Bank and then Arvest Bank Group, the building remained in use until 2006 when it was renovated by the Phillips Petroleum Company. In May 2007, the First National Bank of Bartlesville building became the home to the Phillips Petroleum Company Museum. (Courtesy of the Bartlesville Area History Museum.)

Originally designed to absorb the overflow of students at Bartlesville's College High, Sooner High (now Bartlesville Mid-High) opened in 1967 on the city's east side for students in grades 10 and 11, adding grade 12 a year later. However, its innovative instructional methods as well as exceptional music and drama departments, which held its programs in the facility's 1,019-seat auditorium (shown below), could not guarantee its survival. In 1982, after 15 years, Sooner High's student body was consolidated back into the 1939 art deco–style College High (now Bartlesville High School), and it became home to pupils in grades 9 and 10. (Courtesy of the Bartlesville Area History Museum.)

In 1964, a downtown city block on Jennings Avenue was purchased to make way for a new 24,000-square-foot United States post office. The $650,000 facility, home to 103 employees, 26 mail delivery vehicles, and the origination of 34 postal routes, was dedicated in September 1966 in a ceremony hosted by Mayor William A. Hensley (below), and welcomed visiting dignitaries who also honored the career of Bartlesville postmaster Ernest R. Christopher, who held the position from 1938 to 1966. The single-story post office (above) featured a full basement and its most captivating design element was a zigzag clerestory roofline that marked the main Jennings Avenue entrance as well as a secondary entry on Seventh Street (now Adams Street). (Courtesy of the Bartlesville Area History Museum.)

Bartlesville Public Library & Museum

On November 8, 1989, following a Build a Brighter Tomorrow campaign by the Bartlesville Library Trust Authority, the Bartlesville Public Library closed its doors at the civic center location and relocated to a temporary downtown location pending completion of its new home on an adjacent city block. Demolition of the old library and the civic center began in mid-1990 and groundbreaking for the Bartlesville Public Library and History Museum began in February 1991. The two-story design, by local architect Thomas McCrory in conjunction with Tulsa-based Olsen Coffey Architects, featured a clock tower and state-of-the-art library equipment and catalogue systems. It officially opened with a crowd of nearly 2,500 in February 1992. (Courtesy of Ambler Architects.)

In November 1992, an outdoor sculpture, *The Spirit of Performance*, was unveiled during a dedication ceremony at the Bartlesville Library and History Museum. A gift of the Phillips Petroleum Company and then chief executive office C. J. Silas to honor 75 years of dedicated employee teamwork, the bronze sculpture was executed by Greek-born artist Tasso Pitsiri, pictured, who had worked and taught in Enid and Oklahoma City since 1967. The three figures of *The Spirit of Performance* reach skyward, joining hands, and exemplify not only the performance spirit of Phillips Petroleum employees, but of the Bartlesville community that supported them since 1917. The 1,500-pound work, which began as a small clay model, was unveiled in June 1992, and Pitsiri spent the summer in his Enid studio creating the full-size piece, which is comprised of 12 cast bronze sections welded together prior to the application of a burnished red-gold patina finishing treatment. (Courtesy of the Bartlesville Area History Museum.)

Woolaroc, the ranch retreat for oilman Frank Phillips, was established in 1925 set among the Osage Hills just west of Bartlesville. Its name was derived from the landscape surrounding it—woods, lakes, and rock—and was also the name of the Phillips Petroleum Company airplane, which won the famous Dole Derby, an aerial race from Oakland, California, to Hawaii in 1927. Once retired, the plane's hangar slowly became home to the many Western art objects and Native American artifacts collected by Phillips, and the Woolaroc name soon extended to the entire ranch, and to the subsequent museum of Phillips's collections, Phillips Petroleum artifacts, and local history on the property. In 1999, Woolaroc, and the Frank Phillips Foundation, its governing force since 1944, commissioned the Bartlesville firm of Ambler Architects to design a 3,000-square-foot events center, providing much-needed rental space for meetings, banquets, and catered functions on the ranch property. (Courtesy of Ambler Architects.)

Set within the 3,600-acre Woolaroc wildlife preserve, home to more than 30 varieties of native and exotic animals and birds, the wood-framed Woolaroc Events Center was constructed using materials native to the site, such as the Osage Hills fieldstone on its exterior, which visually connected it to older buildings on the premises. The events center, a short walk from the Woolaroc Museum, Bunkhouse Gallery, and Lodge, was designed by Ambler Architects to include a catering kitchen, restroom facilities, and a large meeting room with stone hearth and exposed wood-beam trusses that provided comfortable seating for groups up to 100. Beyond a wall of floor-to-ceiling windows, an outdoor covered terrace running the entire length of the center was added to give guests spectacular views overlooking the Oklahoma prairie landscape, Clyde Lake and its picnic pavilion, and the neighboring Woolaroc Lodge. (Courtesy of Ambler Architects.)

BIBLIOGRAPHY

Alofsin, Anthony, ed. *Prairie Skyscraper: Frank Lloyd Wright's Price Tower.* New York: Rizzoli, 2005.

Bennett, Joanne Riney. *Pictorial History of Bartlesville.* Bartlesville, OK: Washington County Historical Society, 1972.

DeLong, David G. *Bruce Goff: Toward Absolute Architecture.* Cambridge, MA: MIT Press, 1988.

Dimick, John. *Bartlesville Memoirs.* Bartlesville, OK: Washington County Historical Society, 1982.

Hoffmann, Donald. *Frank Lloyd Wright, Louis Sullivan, and the Skyscraper.* Mineola, NY: Dover Publications, 1998.

Saliga, Pauline, and Mary Woolever, eds. *The Architecture of Bruce Goff, 1904–1982: Design for the Continuous Present.* Munich: Art Institute of Chicago and Prestl-Verlag, 1995.

Weston, Edgar. *Bartlesville Centennial, 1897–1997: Foundations for the Future.* Marceline, MO: D-Books Publishing, 1996.

Williams, Joe. *Bartlesville: Remembrances of Times Past, Reflections of Today.* Bartlesville: TRW Reda Pump Division, 1978.

Woods, Karen Smith. *Bartlesville.* Charleston, SC: Arcadia Publishing, 1999.

Wright, Frank Lloyd. *The Story of the Tower: The Tree that Escaped the Crowded Forest.* New York: Horizon, 1956.

INDEX

Visit us at
arcadiapublishing.com

www.ingramcontent.com/pod-product-compliance
Lightning Source LLC
Chambersburg PA
CBHW080604110426
42813CB00006B/1403